THE NATIVE PROBLEM
IN SOUTH AFRICA

THE NATIVE PROBLEM
IN SOUTH AFRICA

BY

Alexander Davis

WITH A REVIEW OF THE PROBLEM IN

WEST AND WEST-CENTRAL AFRICA

BY W. R. STEWART

(LATE OF THE NIGER COMPANY)

NEGRO UNIVERSITIES PRESS
NEW YORK

Originally published in 1903
by Chapman & Hall, Ltd.   4-9938

Reprinted 1969 by
Negro Universities Press
A DIVISION OF GREENWOOD PUBLISHING CORP.
NEW YORK

SBN 8371-1340-7

PRINTED IN UNITED STATES OF AMERICA

To the Memory of

A DEPARTED STATESMAN

THIS CONTRIBUTION

TOWARDS AN UNDERSTANDING OF A GREAT

SOUTH AFRICAN PROBLEM

IS REVERENTLY DEDICATED

CONTENTS

PART I

THE NATIVE PROBLEM

PART II

MINES AND LABOUR

PART III

WEST AND WEST-CENTRAL AFRICA

THE ANCIENT BARBARIANS

A PARALLEL

THE Germans, in the age of Tacitus, were unacquainted with the use of letters. . . They passed their lives in a state of ignorance and poverty, which it has pleased some declaimers to dignify with the appellation of virtuous simplicity. . . each barbarian fixed his independent dwelling on a spot to which a plain, a wood, or a stream of fresh water, had induced him to give the preference. Neither stone, nor brick, nor tiles were employed in these slight habitations. They were, indeed, no more than low huts, of a circular figure, built of rough timber, thatched with straw, and pierced at the top to leave a free passage for the smoke. . . . the hardy German was satisfied with a scanty garment made of the skin of some animal . . . and the women manufactured for their own use a coarse kind of linen. The game of various sorts, with which the forests of Germany were plentifully stocked, supplied its inhabitants with food and exercise. Their monstrous herds of cattle, less remarkable, indeed, for their beauty than for their utility, formed the principal object of their wealth. A small quantity of corn was the only produce exacted from the earth; the use of orchards or artificial meadows was unknown to the Germans; nor can we expect any improvements in agriculture from a people whose property every year experienced a general change by a new division of the arable lands, and who, in that strange operation, avoided disputes by suffering a great part of their territory to lie waste and without tillage. . . If we contemplate a savage nation in any part of the globe, a supine indolence and a carelessness of futurity will be found to constitute their general character. In a civilised state, every faculty of man is expanded and exercised; and the great chain of mutual dependence connects and embraces the several members of society. The most numerous portion of it is employed in constant and useful labour. The select few, placed by fortune above that necessity, can, however, fill up their time by the pursuits of interest or glory, by the improvement of their estate or of their understanding, by the duties, the pleasures, and even the follies of social life. The Germans were not possessed of these varied resources. The care of the house and family, the management of the land and cattle, were delegated to the old and the infirm, to women and slaves. The lazy warrior, destitute of every art that might employ his leisure hours, consumed his days and nights in the animal gratifications of sleep and food. And yet, by a powerful diversity of nature (according to the remark of a writer who had pierced into its darkest recesses), the same barbarians are by turns the most indolent and the most restless of mankind. They delight in sloth, they detest tranquillity. The languid soul, oppressed with its own weight, anxiously required some new and powerful sensation, and war and danger were the only amusements adequate to its fierce temper. The sound that summoned the German to arms was grateful to his ear. It roused him from his uncomfortable lethargy, gave him an active pursuit, and, by strong exercise of the body, and violent emotions of the mind, restored him to a more lively sense of his existence. . . Strong beer, a liquor extracted with very little art from wheat or barley, and *corrupted* into a certain semblance of wine, was sufficient for the gross purposes of German debauchery. . . The Germans abandoned their immense forests to the exercise of hunting, employed in pasturage the most considerable part of their lands, bestowed on the small remainder a rude and careless cultivation, and then accused the scantiness and sterility of a country that refused to maintain the multitude of its inhabitants. When the return of famine severely admonished them of the importance of the arts the national distress was sometimes alleviated by the emigration of a third, perhaps, or a fourth part of their youth.

GIBBON'S *Decline and Fall of the Roman Empire*

PART I

THE NATIVE PROBLEM

CHAPTER I

INTRODUCTORY

THE great native and labour problem has been troubling South Africa with more or less insistence since the days of native slavery under the Boer. The deprivation of the Boer farmer of the enforced service of the nigger brought trouble very early to the British Administration, and in fact may be deemed the beginning of that bad feeling between the two races which has continued since. Characteristically, the first sign of the fatal breach between Briton and Boer was the direct result of missionary interference in native treatment; we say 'characteristically' without reflection on the present missionary policy, but in the sense that the London Missionary Society of that period exercised the functions of the Aborigines' Protection Society of to-day. As recorded by the historian Mr. Theal, in his 'Progress of South Africa in the Century,' the first exhibition of rancour against the Government resulted from a despatch received by the Governor, Sir John

Cradock, in 1811, from the Secretary of State, enclosing a copy of a letter sent by the Rev. Mr. Read of Bethelsdorp to the directors of the London Missionary Society, complaining that the Hottentots were subject to inhuman treatment by the white people. He asserted that upwards of a hundred murders had been committed in the district of Uitenhage alone, and the horrified Secretary of State demanded a thorough investigation and stringent punishment. This put both the Government officials and the Rev. Mr. Read on their mettle, the Landdrost concerned to show his zeal and obedience, and the Rev. Mr. Read to prove his assertions. Details of this ominous beginning of British interference in Colonial treatment of the native, under the unrestrained and irresponsible influence of religious and philanthropic institutions, are given at length in the chapter dealing with the subject. From that day forward a sharp conflict of feeling has subsisted between those societies in England devoting themselves to the welfare of the native and colonial opinion; in this respect at least Boer and British thought coinciding, though this agreement on the root question failed to prevent the consequent racial estrangement, caused by British apathy and weakness varied with tactless official interference.

History is very apt to repeat itself. In the early days the European inhabitants of the Cape were Dutch either by race or assimilation; it was therefore with these early settlers and voortrekkers that the British authorities had to deal. The final result of a long history of error and weakness combined has been the recent Boer war. To-day British settlement stretches from the Cape peninsula to the Great Lakes, and in any future misunderstanding or conflict over the hardy perennial, Native Treatment, the British authorities will be faced with a united Anglo-Boer resistance.

It is this contingency which occasionally troubles the thoughts of the patriotic South African. In its present phases this unanimity of colonial resistance to British interference in native rule is not apparent on the surface. The cry of forced labour trumpeted against the mining industries of the Rand and Rhodesia suited well the policy of the Boers, giving colour to the deception under which Sir William Harcourt and his following labour, that in their assault on the mining employer on the score of native treatment they enjoy the complete sympathy of the Boer leaders. In the case of Chinese labour, likewise, the Bond and the irreconcilable Transvaaler eagerly join forces with the Natives' Protection Societies in England in hampering and obstructing the development of the mines. But an end to this artificial alliance will soon be reached. During the proceedings of the recent Labour Commission on the Rand it was seen by the evidence of prominent Boers that in opposing Asiatic importation the alternative they suggest approaches forced labour. Botha, De la Rey, Cronje, and others, have not concealed the remedy they have in view, and as this proposed solution directly traverses the principles of Exeter Hall—as the Aborigine Protection sects are termed in South Africa—the Boer population will without question join the British element whenever this conflict in the treatment of the native develops into a real and dangerous issue.

It is with the purpose of forestalling and preventing such a consummation that this book has been written.

It is an endeavour to enlighten the British public on the question, and place before the authorities in power sufficient connected data to enable them to understand the real position in Africa.

Though articles innumerable have been written on the native question, in magazines, in reviews, and in the daily and weekly press ; though we have books by British ' experts' on the native question—men who have examined the question extrinsically and academically—by committees and societies, special pleading, useless sentiment, and patchy attempts at expert information have been fatal obstacles to the proper presentment of the native problem. South African literature is strangely lacking in works comprehensively handling the African native as he actually lives and thinks, and this modest contribution is only advanced as a pioneer effort in this region of inquiry.

To write of the native and the problem he presents some other experience is required than that gleaned in official reports, *ex parte* statements, or academical study. In this, as in most other human problems, it is, if not always essential, still of the greatest advantage, to be in the position to supplement actual study by personal familiarity with the factors presented. And all South African controversies have that peculiarity of demanding a very close and sustained scrutiny before even an approximate judgment can be judicially delivered. South Africa, as we are told, is the 'land of lies '—it might perhaps be more politely termed the land of illusions ; for examining the remarkably divergent views held by different sections of thought, and the absolutely opposed statements on matters of simple fact, one cannot reasonably conclude that the one or the other parties to the controversy are deliberate perverters of truth. It is simply a matter of delusion. It is for this reason that South African questions demand empirical knowledge as well as academical study. Lord Milner was silent for a year, and travelled the land throughout, acquainting himself with the Dutch and their language, before he arrived at a first conclusion and showed his policy, and in this he exhibited great wisdom, as all who refer to his first historic warning to the Dutch in the light of later events will acknowledge. In such a country of pitfalls to avoid a fall one must make oneself acquainted with the ground before careering over the veld, as African travel teaches. There is no precedent, guide, or substitute for South African experience. The problem is not of that sort which may be solved by inductive reasoning or by a study of the past. It is the aim of the succeeding pages to endow the English reader with some basic data upon which to found an approximate conclusion on the Native Question of South Africa, and at the same time to serve to register for the South African in a reasonable compass the heads of the conditions and influences which have to be considered in administering the native and handling the problem.

Affairs in West Africa and the Congo—though the study of the native of these parts has been more closely pursued by competent inquirers than in South Africa, notably in the case of the ever-lamented Miss Kingsley, and by the distinguished native writer Mr. Caseley Hayford, who in writing of his own colour and race possesses unrivalled advantages—have likewise suffered from a redundancy of *British* ‘experts’ upon *Colonial* native affairs. The British public sit at the feet of mentors, having the capacity to specialise and the talent to write, who are comparatively unknown in the land they deal with, either as experts or as practical legislators. Riding on the wave of public opinion and support, they collect in their career all the flotsam and jetsam of varied colonial witnesses, whether reliable or not, whether disinterested or not, and whether known or not. If the bent of their experiences favours the theory these 'experts' profess they are accepted: if the tendency is to moderate or controvert, their authority is either ignored without inquiry or discarded. In this fashion the wave pursues its triumphant course unabated, and public clamour helps its career. Only on the rock of stubborn fact does the wave ultimately break. In this manner the popular impression of native character and treatment becomes entirely distorted, quite out of all knowledge of those who reside on the spot in humble civilian or responsible administrative capacity. The Congo 'atrocities' campaign is fed upon just sufficient a substratum of truth to make it plausible. But the public in their administered sentimentality travel very wide of the true case. After a full career of blood-curdling horrors, unhesitatingly placed at the door of the administrators in highest authority, irrespective of conditions of environment or personal responsibility, a Sir Harry Johnston, of accepted authority, in plenitude of personal knowledge and experience, presents a rock of fact which checks the wave of misrepresentation (see *Daily Chronicle*, Sept. 28).

Sentiment may influence action and dictate policy, but it cannot affect concrete conditions in foreign lands which know it not. In treating native problems it is practical knowledge of existing conditions which serves a useful purpose; sentimental treatment may conceivably do little harm, but almost invariably it does considerable harm. Fortunately all the tremendous influence of British sentimentalism as concentrated in 'Exeter Hall' undergoes the cooling and purifying process of Government departmentalism before it is dealt out for Colonial consumption, else were the Colonial Office a bear garden. As a matter of fact, the clamour rarely indeed is heard further than Downing Street, fortunately.

In the succeeding analytical chapters, the writer examines the native question from the individual standpoint of a strong partiality for the natives, gained by a long period of personal contact, during which many happy days have been spent and good treatment invariably experienced. At the same time, whilst acknowledging a strong bias in favour of the African native, his faults and limitations are rigidly brought to light. In dealing with the problem it is futile to shirk facts, whether telling against the black man or the European. A case shirked in any particular is a case burked, and in nowise a case laid.

CHAPTER II

PRESENT STAGE OF DEVELOPMENT AND MENTAL PLANE

AMID the numerous very knotty problems which present themselves with unfailing regularity in South Africa, and exercise the brains of the most thoughtful of our politicians at home and in the Colonies, the one central factor of deepest root and widest-spread tentacles is the native problem. A Boer is flesh of our flesh ; he is human, accessible, and may be approached through his leaders. The Capitalist has his location as his vocation : the individual swaying the class may be met in Park Lane, in Throgmorton Street, or in Johannesburg. The Afrikander Bond has its Bestuur and the Loyalist League its central executive. Every South African factor in politics, economics, and development has its identity, *ego*, or ' soul ' in personal or corporate presentment except the native. The native problem stands distinct from its rivals in South African study in that it permeates the whole fabric, and to be handled with any success must be grasped in all directions and examined in sections and grades.

In view of the great range of opinion brought to bear upon the native question within the last few years in England it is perfectly natural, almost inevitable, that the average man of intelligence still gropes in hopeless indecision in an honest endeavour to arrive at the truth. When he hears, on the one hand, that the native is subject to treatment only one step removed from slavery, and gathers in another direction that the native is 'coddled,' is hopelessly lazy, ignorant, and stubborn, small wonder indeed that his conclusions swing like a pendulum, just according as the conflicting premises may attract for the time being. And there is little safety in adopting the mean; for the mean in this case would entail the arriving at a conclusion based upon his own premises, and, as in the nature of the case the average man can boast of no expert experience in the subject, the conclusion would have little substance. For among the experts on the native question there are none that take a middle course. We know what South African opinion is on the subject, and we know what 'Exeter Hall' opinion is. Between these two opposed camps is open ground, and no half-way house.

The object of these studies is to supply those taking interest in the subject, some data, culled from first-hand experience, upon which to found an intelligent opinion, and in the first place we will endeavour to briefly sketch the character of the material which has to be dealt with. The political and ethnological history of the Bantu race may be studied by recourse to the standard works and authorities. But to gain any adequate conception of the thoughts, the character, and the personality of the Bantu individual, some other knowledge is required than by reading books, or by merely working with and observing him under a single set of circumstances or peculiar conditions. For instance, a traveller and explorer having many natives for long periods under his control will contend with more or less reason that he understands the 'nigger.' So will the compound manager at the mines and the individual employer. Yet in most cases these authorities on native character are only familiar with the one aspect of many which, taken together, make the 'nigger,' as those who have lived with him *en famille* know him. All estimates of the native are, necessarily, from the outside, for the Bantu has not as yet developed native literature furnishing the student with an inside glimpse of native trend of thought and of character. It is as if our knowledge of the French, or the ancient Romans and Greeks, were merely objective, from our own insular standpoint, and not based in substance on their own literature. The nearest approach to an inner knowledge of native thought and character is that which is acquired by the old native trader and the young Colonial or Boer brought up with and among the natives themselves. Many of this class of European may be found ; but none, as far as we know, have been sufficiently endowed with the necessary qualifications to place their experience and conclusions in graphic form. A virgin field of literature opens out in this direction, portraying Bantu life and thought ; for, though such stories may partake of a more or less apocryphal character, yet, drawn direct from native sources, they cannot fail to shed light on native psychology and volition.

A raw native, undebased by close European contact, is a compound of many elementary virtues and some elementary vices. Where so many different types have developed from a common stock if not common stem, it stands to reason that the one character is not common to all tribes. Yet through all tribes south of the Zambesi of Bantu race a common thread of fundamental character may be traced. Their mode of living has approximated through years of kindred life, though differentiated in detail through diverse influences —migration and wars the forces. Predominating tribes have in their turn yielded to waves of more fierce and warlike predatory stocks.

Yet, throughout, the one vocation common to all has been followed. No branch or tribe of the original element has developed any higher stage of life than the primitive pastoral; many have failed to reach this relatively settled condition. The hoe and the assegai and the native 'piano' are the three highest products of native skill and handicraft evolved through centuries.

The sole remnants of past skill denoting a higher order of being from the Zambesi to the Cape are the ruins of the Zimbabye type, conclusively traced to a people quite distinct from the negro, and almost equally certain to the credit of colonists from other regions, and not to an aboriginal Central or South African race. The one unimportant exception to this absence of a higher cult may be deemed the Bushman's paintings, which in their primitive yet certainly striking and interesting lines and colour merely stand in the nature of an ethnological freak, art developed and lost, perhaps, within a relatively short period. In common with existing and fast disappearing types of aboriginals in North America and Australia, the South African native has never developed even a rudimentary system of written records. The Kafir has no defined religious system, though ethical laws and ethnological observances are fairly general. In fact, as far as the South African aboriginal type is concerned, the one general description in living, thought, and custom applies to every tribe south of the Zambesi.

But, low in the scale of human life as the native may appear, judged by his industrial and intellectual development, any hasty conclusion based upon these premises would probably lead to error. Though intellectually undeveloped, mentally he is robust; that is to say, though intellectually in knowledge of matter and life he is a child, his mental powers are high and above the grade of cunning. He has considerable powers of simple reasoning, and the correctness of his conclusions is only limited by his knowledge. His low intellectual level is mostly due to a lack of imagination and lack of necessity. Shrewd in his estimate of character, he views the wonders of civilisation with a disconcerting nonchalance. Strong in his admiration of physical strength or personal prowess, he will regard the exhibition of a phonograph with stoical demeanour and evanescent surprise, and accept with apparent satisfaction any reasonable or unreasonable solution tendered without further inquiry. All the marvels of civilisation are a one-day wonder to him, and his familiarity with a locomotive or a telegraph dates from his first experience. He would stoke an engine for years without seeking to discover the secret of its working; be taught to take the whole machine to pieces without connecting the piston rod with the steam. Mechanically you could teach him anything, scientifically you would find him a hopeless case. You may teach him to read and write, as many thousands can now read and write; but the writer has never met or heard of a case where anything higher has resulted than facile powers of expression and strong common-sense thought. He lacks imagination.

Physically a native is robust, with strong powers of endurance, yet in feats of unskilled strength he is usually beaten by the robust European. He has great staying powers in running and walking, excelling not so much in speed as in endurance. His physical condition is hard, in the sense that he survives injury to limb where the average European would succumb; but, against this constitutional advantage, he will sink rapidly in cases of organic disease or fevers of an endemic character, even when enjoying good medical attendance. His staple food is farinaceous, and he only kills his cattle on occasions of revel, though from this rule the chiefs are excepted, as the chiefs' kraals are rarely without meat, procured from their own cattle or offerings from dependents. Native fare alternates from a feast to a famine. Though stores are set apart to tide over the periods between the harvests, seldom does foresight instil the prudence of hoarding supplies to meet years of famine, an event of frequent occurrence. The same in minor details; an ox killed is an ox eaten—or, at least, it is by the following morn. In the culinary art the Kafir is not far advanced. The general method of cooking meat is either on a stake, grilled before a wood fire, or boiled in chunks in a great cooking-pot, and eaten with salt. The natives on the East Coast have developed a much higher method of cooking, mainly in the course of many years' contact with the Portuguese. Ground-nut sauce, chillies, tomatoes, and garlic are frequent condiments, and various modes of preparing grain have been acquired from their European masters.

In everyday garb the native is simplicity itself; though on state or ceremonial occasions he loves to

deck himself out in common with human nature.
Some tribes still exist in Northern Rhodesia which go
about stark naked. Mr. Val Gielgud, a Rhodesian
native commissioner, mentions the Abaiyila tribe,
settled along the Kafue River, whose sole pretence to
garb consists of long cones on their heads made of
wool plaited around a horn, some as high as 3 feet
6 inches. The men do not go naked from poverty
but from choice. The natives further south utilise
skins 'brayed' or tanned, prepared bark of trees, and
different varieties of calico, each tribe affecting a particular hue or combination of colours. The Basuto
branch wear loin cloths of scanty dimensions drawn
tightly under the trunk from back of waist to front;
but the Zulu stock affect a more picturesque style in
flowing skins and cloths tied around the loins and
depending back and front almost Highlander fashion.
Iron and brass bangles and anklets are common, some
tribes making a braver show than others. Coloured
rugs, blankets, and shawls are in common use among
all tribes, and the furniture of the household is of the
most primitive description. Wooden head-rests for
pillows, hollowed to receive the neck or head; reed
mats for the floor; pits excavated under the kraal and
structures of reeds and grass upon poles for the grain :
clay pots for cooking, and wooden spoons, practically
exhaust the furniture of a household. The native
weapons of defence consist of the well-known assegai,
of many grades and patterns, some for stabbing and
others for hurling; knobkerries (short stout sticks),
hatchets, and in less dangerous form the staff. Bows
and arrows are practically out of use south of the
Zambesi, except among the sparse and scattered com-

munity of Bushmen. The native huts vary in structure and design according to the tribe. A Zulu or Swazi bee-hive hut of the old stamp is a wonderful structure of strength, patience, and durability. Standing from six to nine feet high and about 25 feet in circumference, it rises symmetrically from the clay floor, its walls a mass of thin saplings bent round to a common centre. These are firmly and closely bound together with an endless ring of plaited grass or bark in concentric circles. Around the exterior, plaited grass is wound, and overlaid with separate rings of the same binding as described above. The structure when completed is waterproof and windproof, strong yet elastic, warm in winter and cool in summer. The one great drawback from an European visitor's point of view is the small aperture which by courtesy is termed a door. An undignified posture of hands and knees is necessary when entering, the unaccustomed crawling in snake-like. There is no chimney or aperture for the escape of smoke, consequently, as a fire is often burning in the neat, round, clay hearth in the centre, asphyxiation rapidly ensues, unless the head is kept on a level with the doorway. By dint of custom, natural selection, or the survival of the fittest, the hardy European whose lot in life leads him among the natives becomes smoke-inured. The native takes it as one of the pleasures of life. The native boasts of no method of illumination, but uses thin dry reeds as a substitute when seeking for an object in the dark hut. Huts of the class described take sometimes over a month to erect, according to the size. Natives on the East Coast have larger and more convenient habitations. These boast of walls of wattle or reed and daub, and high conical roofs. The walls are items of small trouble; but the huge roof is constructed in a similar fashion to the Zulu type of hut, with the one difference that, whereas the Zulu hut is constructed from the base upwards, the Tonga type of habitation is built from the apex outwards. This is accomplished by starting the construction inverted, with the apex on the ground and the saplings radiating from it outwards; the circle is then bound in a homogeneous whole by a process as previously described. When completed, the 'roof' is lifted upon the low, 3-foot walls, which it covers as an extinguisher covers a candle, and rises some ten feet from the level of the ground, forming a convenient shade right around the outside of the hut proper.

In political development the native of to-day presents a decadent tribal system. Along the Zambesi littoral, such as in Barotseland and a few exceptional tracts to the north, between the northern and southern zones of European settlement, a few tribes still enjoy a large measure of their pristine independence; but south of the Zambesi not a tribe remains under independent native control. The systems of government vary from a qualified autonomy in the Bechuanaland Protectorate and in Basutoland, to complete decentralisation in tribal rule such as among the Fingoes and Xosas of the Cape Colony. Native government is now undergoing a rapid course of devolution or disintegration. In Rhodesia the chiefs preside over their tribesmen as paid agents of the Native Department. In Swaziland a hybrid system of dual control prevails. The Zulus of Zululand are policed and governed by Natal Government officials, and in Bechuanaland such enlightened chiefs as Khama and Linchwe govern and

control their tribesmen under the ægis and superinten-
dence of the Protectorate Administration. Basutoland
is under direct Imperial rule, and the chiefs, though
retaining a large proportion of their tribal powers,
are each responsible to the Administrator for the peace
and good government of their particular sphere,
Lerothodi, the nominal paramount, having no means to
enforce his decrees upon his titular subordinates.

Sufficient has been indicated in this very brief
description of native life and present social and political
development to yield a bird's-eye view of the native's
present stage in evolutionary civilisation. As it is seen,
the great mass of raw natives with which we have to
deal at the present time have not yet departed from
their familiar stage of simple but savage life. Though
bereft of their distinguishing features of raider and
raided, of tyrant and victim, of migratory nomad and
submerged slave, yet all the social and much of the
political conditions of yore maintain their ground in
their midst. Instead of being swept by civilisation,
they have but bowed the head, leaving racial entity
and customs still in being though modified to suit the
times.

The tribal system is still kept alive by their white
masters artificially, with the praiseworthy motive of
avoiding a general chaos in the process of devolution
or disintegration. But their persistence is becoming
an anachronism with accumulative force. Chiefs
without authority, princes without land or substance,
a mingling of classes and grades, and a growing
independence of the womankind scarcely conduce to
order, centralisation, or fixity of life and purpose. From
the Cape to the Zambesi may be found natives, kin-

dred in race, colour, and custom, living in all stages of
civilisation and industrial development. Many have
burst the bonds of tribal law, some have joined the ranks
of the Cape half-breeds and Malay Mussulmans. Others
are grouped around Christian missions, while many
have become social nomads drifting where their work
and their masters take them. Zulus and Colony Kafirs
are dwelling among Mashonas and Matabeles—some
thousand miles from their original tribal birthplaces.
Swazis settle in the Transvaal, and Basutos in the
Orange River Colony. Such places as Johannesburg
and Kimberley are great levellers and amalgamators;
while the ports and the towns of the Cape and Natal
are doing their work in training the native labourer to
settled occupation and civilised customs and garb. But
though all these influences are at work, the mass of
natives still remain in pristine ignorance and modified
savagery; acting as the great reservoir from which the
different streams radiate to the industrial centres, but
the drift affecting but little the volume of the main
body, which is always on the increase. It is thus that
when speaking of the 'native' we imply the unit of
the mass and not the emancipated individual of higher
evolution. The latter class is specialised in all refer-
ences and is known by the term *Makolwa*, missionary
boy, or Cape boy—the last term indicating civilised
natives of all grades and shades. As it is said, 'Cape
boy' covereth a multitude of sins, for the popular
meaning of the term in South Africa denotes half-
breeds, including quadroons and octoroons; bridging
in a way the ethnological division between white and
black and other men of colour.

CHAPTER III

NATIVE CHARACTER AND CUSTOMS

THE South African native is frequently compared with a child. This mental estimate inspires the mode of treatment almost universally recommended in dealing with him. Any person experienced in native management will enjoin the necessity of being strict but just, as any weakness of a master or employer is at once taken advantage of, and real kindness or consideration is absolutely wasted. It is an established axiom in colonial circles that natives have no gratitude; that is to say, they will appreciate a just master and seek his service, but an indulgent master can keep no native servant. For instance, if a native be employed at a wage of 2l. per month and works well and his services warrant higher pay, the kind and indulgent master will after a very short time call his servant to him and voluntarily raise his wage. This, as a rule, is a fatal step. The erstwhile industrious and contented worker will at once conclude that he has been cheated; that his services have been underestimated and underpaid. He will stalk the place in gloom, and at the earliest opportunity demand another rise, and yet another rise, until his greed becomes insupportable and the employer loses a good worker. On the other hand, if the employer await a demand for a higher wage and then yield, apparently with much misgivings, the native is delighted and goes about his work with glee, for he has extorted extra pay! By adopting the indulgent attitude you promptly lose your ' boy,' who suspects henceforth every employer; by assuming an attitude of reasonable protest the boy is struck with your justice, and in course of time, as his services appreciate, really obtains full pay without the penalty of becoming spoilt. Gratitude is a virtue which a native does not appear to understand. He will just as lief rob a good master as a bad master—in fact, is much more likely to. A case is recalled where an employer had a young native lad working for him who fell ill. Instead of sending him away back to his people, the youngster was nursed for some weeks and had the privilege of his father visiting him from time to time. Yet directly he got strong he deserted without any pretence, grievance, or compunction. The case is mentioned as typical of the lack of gratitude and stupidity of the raw native. Gratitude is rare among white people, too; but some traces of it are found. Among the natives a case of real gratitude when it occurs—as it might conceivably occur, though during twenty years' experience among natives the writer cannot recall an instance—is ranked as a phenomenon.

But if not grateful a native can be loyal and honest. Treachery in a personal sense is not a marked trait. Outside cases in tribal or native warfare, when many whites have been murdered as a deliberate policy, such as during the Matabele rebellion and during the wars in the Cape Colony and Natal, treachery is rare. Against the murders committed in times of war numerous cases may be recalled where Europeans residing in native territory have been warned and their lives spared. In times of peace the trader and the pioneer living among the natives have been, with few exceptions, as safe as, and even safer than, they would be in London. In Zululand, Basutoland, and Swaziland cases of violence against European residents since the earliest period of contact have been few and exceptional. As a matter of fact, despite his savage and chequered history, the native is eminently law-abiding. Accustomed to the stern justice of tribal law and blind obedience to authority, he accepts the rule of the European with the same exhibition of tractability.

It is a native privilege to lie. It is more. It is a virtue. It is an act of politeness. Among Europeans to be polite some variation from the truth is necessary. Should a homely kind of a young woman ask with gaping smile if she looks fair, you gallantly respond, 'Oh, yes.' A native will praise his chief to the skies and laud his virtues to the heavens. Such flattery is known among Europeans; but a native will drive the principle to its logical conclusion. If you ask for food he will politely declare that he is starving, though food in abundance is in sight. He will lie with the truth staring you both in the face and affect surprise, but no discomfiture, upon being confronted with proof of his mendacity. He will tell you his cousin is his brother, his mother is his wife, and his nephew is his child with solemn persistency, and the onus of proof lies with you. He will just as readily lie without purpose as with purpose. His lies, as a rule, are more constitutional than malicious. In South African courts of justice the magistrates have a difficulty to penetrate to the truth in native cases. A case once occurred at Salisbury, Rhodesia, where a native charged another with knocking him down and robbing him. His story ran that he went to an eating-house kept by the defendant and innocently asked for change for 1*l*., whereupon walking out he was set upon, knocked down, and robbed of 4*l*. He had his witnesses. His first witness swore that he and the defendant were gambling at cards, and that the plaintiff lost 1*l*. 10*s*., and then snatched the prisoner's money, on which the prisoner knocked him down and recovered it. Every witness brought in support made the complainant's case look blacker. The magistrate dismissed the case in despair. In most native trials the wisdom of a Solomon is essential, and as such wisdom is granted to few men many a native escapes justice and many suffer from injustice owing to their unfortunate propensity for lying.

In war all is fair among natives. The victor has the spoil and does not spare the vanquished. The Kafir certainly comes from a warlike, pitiless, and unrelenting stock. But torture as a fine art, in the sense of the primitive Red Indian, is not a custom. Mutilations are occasionally resorted to as a special punishment, and death by binding to an ant-heap has been heard of, but as a rule the tyrant and the conqueror deal death quick and sure. Stabbing with assegais and clubbing with knobkerries or axes are the general mode of slaughter for man and beast. When a kraal is doomed to destruction it is surrounded silently on break of day, and the people slaughtered as they leave or flee the huts. In open warfare, before firearms were possessed, much display of individual braggadocio preluded the impact of forces. The native exhibits bravery in varied intensity according to the tribe, though even the meanest tribe on emergency, especially under sound leadership and when fanaticism is aroused, develops rare courage. Witness the desperate struggle of the despised Mashonas during the Matabele rebellion. This case also exhibits the lack of gratitude inherent in natives. The Mashonas were oppressed for years by the Matabele, and rescued from servitude by the Chartered Company; yet at the first opportunity they rose against their benefactors and joined their late oppressors! But despite this tendency to destroy all that cross their path when on the raid, and the many evidences of courage that may be collected, the natives, when faced on equal terms with one another, are not prone to great destruction. Many of their so-called battles have been farces, and their propensity for exaggeration may be recalled as prominent in their accounts of actions during the late Boer war. On one occasion a trial was held at Eshowe, in Zululand, over a faction fight. Said one of the witnesses, 'We came out of the reeds and we poured down on them with our assegais. We fought and we fought; we killed and we killed; we stabbed and we stabbed.' The judge, horror-stricken, turned to the interpreter and said, 'Ask him how many men were killed?' 'One,' was the reply. Similarly in Pondoland. Sigcau, the paramount chief, was at loggerheads with one of his minor chieftains, and they met in open conflict just on the Natal borders. A detachment of Natal police watched the fight from the heights with orders to stop combatants from crossing the border. The fight lasted with varying success all the day, and the result, as far as was ascertained, was one man drowned by accident !

Though love, in the poetic sense, appears dormant or absent in the native, yet affection is a prominent trait, although it has peculiar limitations. For instance, the love of the parent for offspring is marked, and the respect of children for their parents is a pleasing trait in native family life; but when the parties get old, unless their station be high, little care or attention is wasted upon them. They become neglected and dirty, which condition is, perhaps, in some cases, the result of their own growing contempt for appearances. Cases are known where chiefs, even while nominally still exercising authority, degenerate into the most pitiful objects in the kraal. Grey hairs among men, at least, are respected, especially while the intellect remains unclouded. A good deal of flirting is carried on among the young of both sexes, but immorality, in the technical sense of the word, is rare. There is much more of real modesty among the maidens than false modesty. Clad in scanty garb, there is no thought of shame, but among the unsophisticated tribespeople the advent of a white man in their midst is conducive to more raiment. As bearing upon this subject of covering the form, it is noteworthy that the European very quickly becomes accustomed to the native simplicity of garb, and that which at first appears strange and savage very soon becomes familiar and natural, so much so that, by dint of familiarity, a native girl ill or thinly clad from head to foot looks more indecent and more vulgar to one accustomed to kraal life than a maid with only a string of beads around her loins. Carlyle could have added some chapters to this subject.

That conjugal love of a high order does exist among
the natives of the kraal is shown by the following
veracious circumstance. At Bulawayo one Senkane,
a native residing in the Bulilima-Mangwe district, had
occasion to quarrel with his wife. His brother, who
was present, strove to patch up the quarrel, but was
told not to interfere, as it did not concern him. During
the night the woman disappeared, and in the morning
her husband and the brother searched for her. Her
body was found suspended by a calico cord to a tree in
the mealie garden—an evident case of suicide. Senkane,
greatly distressed, declared that the quarrel was over
nothing, and became prostrated with sorrow. He
asked his brother to go and acquaint his wife's father
of her death. The brother departed, and when he
returned he found the body on the ground, but not the
rope, and near the scene the unfortunate and devoted
husband was discovered to have hanged himself in a
fit of deep remorse and grief. Such an incident is
extremely rare, but shows that, after all, colour is but
skin deep where human passion is concerned.

Laziness is a popular charge made against the
native. From a modern and civilised standpoint he is
lazy. He has as much disinclination to work with the
sweat of his brow at industrial pursuits as we have to
grasp an assegai and set out for a hundred-mile tramp
on a raiding expedition. In the halcyon days of independent rule the chiefs were the leisured classes, just
as among ourselves. The *umfaans*, or lads, herded
and tended the cattle. The bigger youths and young
bloods were occupied unceasingly in raid and defence,
in chase and in building, in clearing bush and in skilled
handiwork. The ruling castes were soldiers and the

conquered were slaves, except in those cases where they became incorporated and absorbed in the ranks of their tyrants. Tramps of fifty and one hundred miles were frequent in the days when raiding and killing, spying and despatch carrying, were proper, manly vocations. The men were called up by their chiefs for personal service, and, in addition, managed and controlled the cattle given to their care and owned by them in person. Now the bulk of this work has disappeared. As the need of procuring food remains, and the women did the tilling and tended the field, the female lot is neither lightened nor ameliorated, while the males find their occupations gone. The personally or hereditarily idle native, while he has his womenfolk to administer to his needs, will not go far afield or move from his doorstep to procure wealth. Those that have higher ambitions and are of an adventurous nature, or are driven by domestic necessity, repair to the distant centres and procure the wherewithal to purchase what they desire. Many have recourse to work from sheer necessity to obtain money to pay the *lobolo* for a wife or additional wives and then settle down to native repose, when they simply vegetate and remain in the savage and ignorant conditions so dear to the hearts of their protectors in England. Others, from a love of the life at the mine or in the settlement, bound by influences to which they become attached, or from avarice or ambition, remain at their work for long periods and return after a brief visit to their homes. The latter class of native is the one which forms the backbone of mine labour. But their proportion to the mass is a small one. It is thus seen that from a civilised point of view the native is fundamentally lazy, and even in his more congenial occupations more labour than necessary for the time being is an abomination to him. In a report by a Native Commissioner of the Sebungwe District of Northern Matabeleland it is stated of the natives of those regions that they are terribly lazy, and during the heat of day generally go to sleep. If you go over their fields along the river you will find the crops being destroyed by the locusts while the natives are asleep, and not the slightest attempt is made to clear them off. Further, they are extremely improvident. There are a number of indigenous fruits which are palatable, and to save themselves the trouble of climbing the tree and gathering the fruit they cut the tree down. Along the river bank crops can be grown all the year round, and with the local fruits and a certain amount of fish they are able to live. It is this wonderful fertility of the soil that makes them so lazy, as they can always live from hand to mouth. But it must be said that this laziness and improvidence are not without their exceptions among the tribes. The Basutos are large farmers and export a great amount of grain. Tribes in the Northern Transvaal, in the Lydenburg district, are also large grain growers, but these exceptions prove but the rule. The native, generally speaking, certainly fails to make the most of his opportunity.

The religion of the Bantus consists of a rudimentary system of ancestor-worship. They believe in spirits and ghosts, and in cases have family and tribal totems, but judged by the terms of the most sacred oaths departed chiefs are the ideals mostly held in reverence. The arrival of some Angoni (a Zulu offshoot) headmen at Zomba, British Central Africa, in April 1898, was taken advantage of by examining them in respect to their customs and belief. They denied any knowledge of the existence of a God, and thought that after a man died the grave marked the end of his identity; yet they believed in ghosts. They had no tradition as to the origin of the human race. In an interesting description of the Mang'anga and A'Chipata tribes of Zambesia which appeared in the *Rhodesian Times* of February 4, 1899, the natives are said to believe that man and the animals first came to earth by falling down a sloping rock whose sides still show the marks of descent. 'An idea of God (Mulunga) is present among the people to account for this fall. The village often has a special hut attached where prayers are said either to avert some calamity or to invoke some benefit for the people. There are no special priests, the chief, as temporal head of the people, officiating in their stead. The nether world with them is the grave and its power the spirits of the departed. The spirits of the dead are believed to exercise a ruling influence over the destinies of the living, and it is to them that the people pray. Thus the idea of God perishes before the spirits, and the spirits themselves end in nothingness, for they have no conception of a universal and eternal resurrection, or of the immortality of the soul. Thus their religion is nothing more than a few hypotheses invented to account for natural phenomena, and their beliefs have no deeper foundation than is found in the ghost stories of primitive superstitious peoples. Prophets are said to exist, but they are rather the mouthpieces of the spirits than of any Supreme Being.' As throwing additional light on native

superstitions and beliefs a traveller in the Awemba
country, a territory north of the Zambesi River under
the Chartered Company, describes the custom on the
death of a chief. 'His near relatives kill his wives
and slaves, and the chief lies unburied in the house
where he died for about a year, his body being guarded
by some of his most faithful headmen. Beside the
body are placed his ivory and a quantity of cloth—the
native bark cloth and trade calico and fancy stuffs.
At the end of the year the body is taken to the district
of " Mharuli " and buried with great ceremony, there
being again a slaughter of women and slaves. The
body is placed in a sleeping posture and covered with
blankets or calico, or bark cloth, and a hole is cut
above the right ear in the cloth. On being asked the
meaning of this custom one is told that the chief is
not dead, he is sleeping; one day the *Mlungu* (God)
will call him and this hole is to let him hear the voice
of the *Mlungu* quickly.' 'Another custom of the
Awemba and other tribes to the west is divination by
the ordeal of the "Zambia." A native (generally a slave)
is taken, bound, and his throat cut and an instrument
placed to the wound; the arterial blood spouts into this
instrument with a weird whistling sound, and it, on
being filled up, is over-balanced and rings a bell and
omens are drawn accordingly.' It is interesting to
note that *uhmlungu* is the generic name given by
natives in South Africa to Europeans, thus denoting
their high estimation of the power and origin of the
white man.

Since their contact with whites the natives throughout the land—Christian and Pagan—have a conception
of the *Inkos Inkulu* (the Great Chief), *Inkosi Pazulu*

(God above)—terms used in expressing the God of Christianity; but their reverence towards this deistic conception is based upon the logic that, just as the European is superior to the ˙black in all arts and sciences, so must the God of the European be superior to their own spirits. Their ethical system—and they have their 'ethical as ethnological laws—has no visible connection with inspiration, but is rather the result of custom and policy. A fine paid may condone almost any offence, though capital punishment is often resorted to. The *Inyangas, Molimos*, or witch-doctors, are the mediums between the living and the departed, and wax rich on their nefarious traffic. They make it their business to discover all the hidden springs of action and the scandal of their environment. They become sooth-sayers and detectives; witch-finders and spirit-baiters. They use others as their tools and become tools themselves in their turn, as circumstances develop. A favourite method of divination is by 'throwing the bones'—a bagful of dirty charms, such as small knuckle bones, bits of herb, and queer stones. At a *séance* of this description the witch-doctor sits with a circle of the people around him, or himself forms one of the circle. These 'bones' are then gathered up into the closed palms of the two hands and cast suddenly on the ground; then the witch-doctor peers and scans their position. As he consults the oracle he delivers a kind of commentary, while his audience loudly shout at all his remarks, *Si Ya Vuma!* ('We agree'). As he pro-ceeds the *Si Ya Vuma*, accompanied with a snapping of fingers, increases in vehemency, until the right thing is said and the desired object gained, when the 'doctor' departs with his reward. On one occasion in

Swaziland a European trader lost from his stock a box of percussion caps. They were stolen from a waggon. All the natives of the adjacent kraal were summoned and the loss made known, together with a demand for the culprit. But all stoutly denied the theft. The trader, therefore, sought a witch-doctor and employed his services to find what had become of the missing property. A *séance* was held to which all the men were summoned and the ' bones ' were thrown. After two *séances* the witch-doctor announced amid the plaudits of his audience that he had discovered the missing property and indicated the place where the box was to be found. Sure enough the property was there. In rewarding the ' doctor ' the trader promised him an extra guerdon if he would disclose the means of his discovery. A bargain was struck, whereupon said the ' doctor,' he found after sundry manœuvring that one of his audience was not so hearty in his *Si Ya Vumas* as the rest, and he fastened the theft on him by repeated innuendos, only appreciated by the suspected one. After the first *séance* the culprit stealthily sought the ' doctor ' in fear and trembling and acknowledged the theft. The rest was easy. But the ' doctor's ' reputation had been established by the wonderful quality of his divining powers. On similar lines to these most of the witch-doctors' reputations are built. Their business is to discover the hidden lives of their people, to which task they diligently devote themselves. When, as sometimes occurs, a victim is marked down for destruction a case is easily worked up against him by the aid of the witch-doctor.

But the witch-doctor's cunning is exercised in other and more repellent directions. Among the Batshangane, a tribe now brought more directly under Portuguese rule since the defeat and capture of King Ngungunyama, during the periodical war dances it was the custom of the witch-doctors to slay a boy and a girl of tender years, mix their blood with that of an ox, and use the 'muti' as medicine to 'doctor' the young braves. 'Smelling out' used to be an established practice with all the tribes of South Africa. This was in most cases accomplished with the 'bones,' as previously described, and the victim in most cases was marked down for destruction before the ceremony—a victim of jealousy, of avarice, or revenge ; but, doubtless, in some instances also an evil-doer. Ordeals of various kinds were common practices among the tribes, and are probably resorted to to-day among those tribes not in close contact with the white man. For instance, in an ordeal by poison a victim is made to drink a vegetable poison. If he is sick and vomits the poison he is deemed 'not guilty'; should he retain the poison, among some tribes the victim was clubbed to death, anticipating the action of the deadly potion.

In an account given in the *Central Africa Times* of Blantyre the gross imposture and crass stupidity of the witch-doctor and his dupes were clearly exposed by a trader. A native was charged with theft, and a witch-doctor called in to try him. Surrounded by an awe-struck audience, the 'doctor,' amid the low beating of drums, placed a pot upon a fire, in which some mwavi bark was steeped. He chewed some small pieces of straw, took the pot off the fire, and appealed to the spirits. He then spat in the pot, and only a slight fizzing resulted. 'That proves it,' said the

doctor (reminiscent of ' Alice in Wonderland'). The
question was then asked by the trader if in any case
such a result would not have happened. ' Oh, no ! '
said the witch-doctor, and he then proceeded to show
how in another trial the effect of the straws was to
make the decoction effervesce and steam away. But
the trader discovered the secret. In one case the pot
remained on the fire until the end of the oration, and
in the other the pot was taken off until the decoction
cooled. The trader then proceeded to show how a rat
could be found guilty of the same crime, and did so.
But the natives took this exposure in characteristic
fashion. It did not destroy their confidence in their
own witch-doctor, but only established the greater fame
of the trader. But the accused's life was saved.

Witchcraft, even in its most hideous form, still
retains a hold among the general run of natives, even
those dwelling amid civilised communities. A case is
recorded at Harding, Natal, about four years ago,
wherein one Umtanti, a witch-doctor, and three other
natives confessed to the murder of a resident, Mr.
James Kay, for the purpose of procuring medicine
from the white man's body. The plan for the murder
had been concocted weeks before. It was arranged
to pounce upon the white man during the ploughing
season, when all his servants would be away. Gomfi
and Umbonwa, two of the accused, had portions of a
native woman that had been killed (a relation of Chief
Remshwe), and a white man's flesh was required to
mix with the same. Umtanti was to be well paid for
mixing the medicine, which was to act as a love
philtre. Umtanti stated that Government were quite
right in hanging him, and that he wished his con-

fession to be conveyed to Mr. Kay's relations in England, asking their forgiveness. The execution was carried out without a hitch in the presence of the chiefs and headmen of the district. After the bolt was drawn the native chiefs were invited to see the bodies as they hung, and again when in their coffins, thus providing an impressive object-lesson.

Rainmakers are specialities in every tribe—in some cases the chiefs are hereditary rainmakers and in others some famous witch-doctor. The kings of Swaziland were of the former kind, and their reputation ranged far and wide, beyond their own tribal boundaries, extending to Zululand and the Shangaan country. In times of drought the afflicted people sent copious presents to the royal rainmaker. Should the heavens be kindly and send down their treasure much jubilation took place, and the king's praises were sounded. Should the heavens be obstinate and withhold their waters, then the presents were insufficient and further gifts poured in. In cases of severe drought the people were wicked and much ' smelling out ' took place to find the witches. In any case the king scored, and his reputation remained intact. All very illogical, but founded upon Faith—upon which most other religious beliefs are founded. In the interview with the Angoni chiefs previously referred to, they described their rainmaker as a woman. She was married, but the husband did not share her skill. They lived together during the dry season, and when the rains came on they parted. Her house was full of snakes and medicine for making rain. It appears her reputation was first established by the fact that when she was captured in a raid there were torrents of rain, though it was the dry season. This she evidently took advantage of, and volunteered to make a shower on her own account, and she did it. The headmen brought her a black goat and four yards of blue cloth each, and she 'rained' until they wanted it stopped. She could also 'thunder and lightning' and make 'hailstones.' When she tied a strip of white calico round her head the rain stopped at once. When it failed to rain she was busy 'making' it; when it rained too much she was busy stopping it. To the awkward question as to her method when one wanted rain and the other did not, it was averred that she arranged it to suit both.

Typical of the obstinate belief of the natives in their traditional superstitions, despite contact with white men and the cessation of the witch-doctors' baneful rites due to the presence of the European, is the complaint of an old Swazi to an interviewer at Bremersdorp. 'Is it for our good,' he said, 'that our King should not be allowed to kill witches who travel through the country and sow poison in our gardens that we get no crops, or put medicine in our beer that we drink and get sick and die, or put charms on the road so that the girls who walk along the path get bewitched and run away from home, and we lose the lobolo? That is not good. The country will go to the bad.' This lament seems almost an echo of the 'good old days' of civilised life. Among the superstitious natives it is very unwise to hold any particular personal article of a neighbour. More especially does this danger operate should any animal tissue of a living person be discovered. Natives are careful to burn their nail-parings, torn skin from wounds, hair, or any attribute or portion of the body discarded. Even portions of apparel and close personal adornments found in the possession of another inspire a suspicion of witchcraft. A story is told of the Angoni chief, Mpezeni, to whom came two half-castes on trading bent. Summoned to the King's hut, after some conversation the chief went outside for a moment, during which period one of the half-castes innocently handled one of the royal rugs, tearing out some hairs. This act was observed by one of the wives present, and when the King returned she acquainted him of what had passed during his absence. The King, in fear of becoming bewitched, had the man dragged out and promptly executed.

The witch-doctor also dispenses medicine and charms. A very fruitful study awaits the herbalist who shall direct his researches to the properties of South African plants and the medicinal system of the natives. A Kafir doctor, to the uninitiated, with his mummeries of dress and practice, cuts but a sorry figure, and presents all the appearance of imposture and mendacity. To those better acquainted with the lives and activities of the Kafirs in their tribal state, underlying the mass of ignorance exposed to the surface is a substratum of knowledge much of which still remains unrevealed to the learned and cultured specialist of more civilised races. The native doctor performs a great many other operations than divining, ' smelling out,' and slaying. Many of these dirty-looking horrors are deeply versed in herbal lore and acquainted with the properties of herbs of which our savants have but the slightest knowledge. The use made of this knowledge is often for evil, but some-times for good ; and many a stranded pioneer and hunter, wounded and lying ill on the veld, has been thankful for assistance rendered in places and at times when no better skill is available. Sometimes these native remedies fail egregiously, as in a case reported at Bulawayo, where a man and a girl both died from potions administered by the local ' doctor ' for the cure of dysentery. Sometimes the remedy is regarded by the European as worse than the disease, as happened in Swaziland, where a trader lying prostrate from malarial fever and desiring an emetic from the native ' doctor ' had a large washbasinful of green liquor placed before him with the injunction to swallow the lot! As the old adage says, ' One swallow does not make a summer,' and in this particular instance one swallow also failed, and the stricken pioneer let it pass—and recovered by the mere threat of the great green evil-smelling dose. A similar case occurred in Namaqualand, where some Bushmen were tried by the authorities for murder. According to the dramatic sequel it appears that the deceased travellers had innocently asked for food, and the Bushmen good-naturedly proffered them certain roots to cook and eat. The result was death. The properties of these herbs killed the Europeans, but nourished the Bushmen. In the days of the laager, during the Matabele rebellion, rumour stated the natives brought their knowledge of poisons to practical use by infecting the waters of the commonage, and thus causing the death of many horses and cattle. That poisons are used by the evil-disposed among the natives is common knowledge, although the practice is one which is condemned by native law, and when used is generally for spite or revenge rather than for gain.

Native women, as is customary among polygamous races, do not stand on equality with the men. Nearly

all the agricultural labour at a kraal is performed by
women. But native women are not the slaves they
are universally accounted to be. The native woman,
generally speaking, not only does not work under
protest, but would protest if the work were taken from
her charge and undertaken by the other sex. She
tills the soil, gathers the grain, and carries the water—
sometimes a task in itself of considerable magnitude,
when, as often occurs, the water supply is situated a
mile or so from the kraal—and is withal not unhappy
in her lot, or a mere cipher in domestic control. At
the present day, when conditions are changed and the
native warrior becoming extinct as a class, the evil of
the system is not so much that the women work too
hard as that the man works too little. The native
women while administering to their lord and master
possess many privileges. Their labour is not enforced
labour. They have a distribution of their earnings,
nothing is 'pooled' or arbitrarily disposed of, and
the very marriage customs are not such a matter of
barter as popularly imagined. Domestic life in a kraal
has little to gain from civilisation in gaiety and
happiness. The very aged, though not ill treated, are
neglected, it is true; but the young are well treated
and well disciplined, and the elders are regarded
with becoming respect. Each wife has her personal
belongings and her own family circle within the household. Over all presides the husband and father, whose
authority is just as much dependent upon his character
and his firmness as among ourselves.

Occasionally great jealousy exists in a household
between the wives, and cases are frequent, where the
husband is unwise enough to exhibit marked preference

for one of his spouses, for the other to make his life a
burden. Yet the husband can be the tyrant when he
chooses and has the nerve and spirit to command.
Chastisements are known, but not common. A circumstance is recalled of an incident which occurred at a
young chief's kraal in Swaziland. Hanyan was a very
' big pot' indeed, being the rightful heir to Msila's
throne of the Bashangaans, then occupied by Gungunhana. He and his followers took shelter in Swaziland, under the protection of King Umbandine. Two
European traders, with whom he was very friendly,
became very merry with his wives, a bevy of handsome
young women, during his absence one day. It was
innocent fun, but when the chief returned he took
umbrage, and much to the traders' dismay had all his
wives thrashed. Such a harsh measure, however, is
very exceptional among natives, the native women,
as a rule, having perfect liberty to laugh and chaff
with those with whom they are acquainted, and very
rarely indeed among natives in their savage state
does this intercourse result in a breach of chastity.
In an account of the natives in the Kafue district
of Northern Rhodesia, Mr. Val Gielgud gives a
peculiar variant from the common custom of natives
in their domestic habits. He says that among the
Abaiyila when a married man is about to depart on
a journey he says to a friend, ' Here are my huts,
my cattle, my grain, and my wives; will you look
after them for me?' When he departs his friend
looks after these possessions, the wives included, and
should the result of this be that a woman becomes
enceinte, then she remains with her temporary husband
till the child is born and weaned.

One of the most peculiar and essential customs in native polity, tending to keep the communists intact, tending to morality, to industry, and to communal responsibility, is 'lobolo.' The principle upon which this custom is based is that a father losing the services of his child—girls and women performing all the household duties—is entitled to some equivalent before he transfers these advantages to another. At first glance, superficially, this exchange of bride and cattle has all the appearance of barter, of sale of a girl to the first-comer. But in essence and practice it is nothing of the kind. It must not be imagined that a female child or dependent is regarded and treated as a slave. Far from it. The girl often refuses consent, and is seldom arbitrarily dealt with. If pressure is attempted, the girl has the means of making matters generally uncomfortable. But, as a matter of fact, genuine parental and filial affection is very strong among Kafirs, and the parent and the girl are both as a rule united in the desire to attach themselves to a rich suitor, the age and appearance of the prospective relative seldom being of great consequence. 'Lobolo' is hedged round with various safeguards. Should a wife desert her husband or prove untrue the dowry has to be returned. Provision is also made in the case of a love or runaway match—should the parent relent and not demand a fine or the return of the bride—for payment of dowry to be deferred until such times as children bless the union, when these treasures are retained by the grandfather as hostages. If the wife is ill treated and she desert to her father's home, the husband runs the risk of losing both wife and the cattle he may have paid for her. In former times wives were often obtained by the raid of the maiden from the enemy or by the capture of cattle ; but now, under a settled government, either cattle or cash has to be acquired, inherited, or earned. This operates in favour of an incentive for the native to work, and provides a sound argument in this sense for its retention. Owing to the new conditions entailing the loss of prestige and power by the chiefs, the ' lobolo ' custom has greatly weakened, and is much evaded and ignored, with the result that much immorality, hitherto unknown, and promiscuous marriages, easily entered into and easily terminated, have been prevalent, to the disgust and dissatisfaction of the elders of the native communities—which ill effect is another argument in favour of retention. Such a law, pending civilisation becoming general—and Christian natives are exempt—operates advantageously both from a social and an economical standpoint. The subject, however, has aroused much controversy, some authorities leaning to the view here adopted, and others— notably the missionary class—contending that polygamy should be discountenanced, if not abolished. Bishop Gaul, of Mashonaland, in giving his views on the subject, has declared that polygamy militates against habits of industry. For, he contends, as long as wives are mere property and can be bought at so much per head, and are mere burden-bearers and menial breeders of daughters for the marriage market, the native will never be made to believe he ought to work for work's sake. The Bishop says that polygamy only encourages him to work a little in his youth in order that he may fatten on the labour of his wives in his full manhood and thrive by the sale of his daughters. The right reverend gentleman would treat the possession of more than one wife as a decided luxury, and all receipts from the sale of a daughter as a source of income to the State. A sense of citizenship would be gradually developed, and labour would become a necessity to the man and household duties to the woman. Against this opinion may be urged that, although in theory polygamy is depraving, yet in practice among the savages, before a better system is evolved, it is better to keep to old and restraining lines than break down the barriers prematurely and thoughtlessly before another protection is ready to take their place. If polygamy were unrecognised by Government or disallowed before Christianity had taken hold, then the risk would be run of a great access of immorality among the derelicts with ties unloosened. The subject has recently been considered and dealt with by the Rhodesia Government, and the resulting regulations adopted have interest as being the latest issued in South Africa on the subject, based upon those still extant in Natal and the Cape Colony. It is provided that in future no lobolo, whether of stock or its equivalent in other property, or payment in cash, shall be given for a period of more than twelve months prior to the marriage, and lobolo given at any earlier period shall in no case be recoverable. In order to check the greed of a parent and keep the lobolo within proper bounds, limits are set to demands. In the case of a girl or woman being a daughter of a chief in charge of a tribe, five head of cattle or cash equivalent; all other natives, four head of cattle or the equivalent in property or cash. And the cattle are not to be valued higher than 5l. per head. It is set out that when it is desired that a marriage shall be contracted between natives the parties thereto and the father or guardian of the girl or woman, together with the chief of the tribe or a headman deputed by the chief, shall appear before the Native Commissioner, who is a local magistrate. He shall satisfy himself that lobolo in accordance with the provisions of the Ordinance has been delivered to the satisfaction of the parties concerned, and shall obtain from the girl or woman who is a party to the contemplated marriage her personal consent. The Administrator has powers to suspend the Ordinance in those districts where there are no European centres of control.

The native system of rule among Kafirs is a qualified tyranny—a tyranny tempered with revolt, assassination, and intrigue—much as has been the case with tyrants among their white masters. The king or paramount chief of a tribe is a very big man indeed, physically and potently. Physically because among the tribes, and especially among that branch of which the Zulu nation is the best known, a chief with any kind of pretence to majesty must be big of frame and great of paunch. Naturally all chiefs are not so well favoured as, for instance, the late Cetchwayo ; but Lobengula of Matabele fame, and Umbandine of Swazi history, ran the Zulu king very close in proportions. The power of the paramount chief was measured (for we may talk of him as of the past) by his determination, cunning, or bloodthirstiness. The claim that he was guided by his councillors and could do little without their consent is hardly borne out by actual history. Neither of the three chiefs here mentioned would brook opposition by any councillor, or, as a matter of fact, any faction of his tribe. Really the only remedy a groaning and dissatisfied nation had against their king was intrigue and poison. And this for a very simple reason. It was the king alone who had a standing army, and the warriors were too eager to flesh their spears in any bloody work to give much heed to any but the man who fed them and kept them employed at congenial vocations. In him was vested supreme power. He was the high fount of justice, commander-in-chief, and in many cases the supreme witch-doctor and invested with as much divine attribute as native belief permitted. In some tribes he has, or perhaps we should say had, the sole privilege of inflicting death; but many of the great native tribes included within their system tributary chiefs who claimed this right over their own vassals. In questions of national importance the chief summoned to his assistance a council of the leading headmen; but in the case of a masterful chief this aid was more from motives of finding a scapegoat peradventure failure result than from any burning sense of mutual dependence.

Lost prestige and weakness alone have been the undoing of fallen chiefs. Said Cetchwayo once to a visitor who mildly chided him on his bloodthirstiness, ' Look here, my friend. Just come and rule my people for a week, and if you do not incline to kill them all I will eat my head '—or words to that effect. The ' king's kraal ' of these past autocracies was a hotbed of intrigue—not intrigue against the king, but faction disputes and a rush for favours. ' Killing off ' for witchcraft was almost a daily proceeding. Little parties of the king's bodyguard were sent almost daily to different portions of the kingdom to do their dread work of massacre. Sometimes the punishment was deserved and sometimes the result of jealousy, greed, or spite of neighbours. Occasionally, when the quarry was a noble and powerful one, secret warning was given, when preparations for defence were made while the doomed chieftain and his men got their cattle together to flee the slaying horde. In this fashion Msiligaazi escaped from Chaka and founded the Matabele nation in the Transvaal, emigrating subsequently to present Rhodesia, his path strewn with slaughtered indigenes. The native chief has many wives; one his royal wife, from whom the heir was generally chosen, others his 'right' and 'left hand' wives, and many concubines. A native court differs but little in effect from others where polygamy is the custom. Petty jealousies, intrigue, and very often crime abounded in the royal enclosure. The king himself, as in the case of the minor chiefs, was generally distinguished by the common attributes of gentle birth. A nobler mien, a softer skin, and smaller hands and feet than the common herd marked them from their surroundings. The royal maidens, especially of the Zulu and Swazi courts, were very fine specimens of humanity. Many are favoured with handsome features, by no means negroid, and their forms might well serve as models for a Juno or a Venus. Wherever the paramount chief travelled a great retinue of attendants and soldiers accompanied him, and where he rested food and beer had to be provided by his subservient hosts.

The native induna, or councillor, is a typical aristocrat of the satrap type, combining, often, the office of king's privy councillor. At his own kraal and when residing in his own domains he exercises almost royal authority among his own people; when stationed at the king's kraal he acts as the king's deputy, receives deputations, judges cases, and generally relieves the great chief from the routine of governing. But in most cases his office is no sinecure or a permanency, and carries with it a large amount of personal risk. Intrigue might any day undo him, and years of faithful service to his master will not save him from the extreme penalty when the exigencies of the times call for his ' wiping out.' One of the wisest councillors of a native king coming under the writer's notice was the great Sandhlan, the chief induna or prime minister of Umbandine, King of Swaziland. This great and wise chief had served the king's father, M'Swazie, before him, and was regarded by the nation as the father of the people. He resided in the largest kraal in the kingdom, a short distance from the king's kraal, in which place in the course of many years he had gathered around him a great native city, all owing him allegiance and living in security under his immediate sway. Sandhlan had a prodigious memory, which in a land where no written records were kept proved of great service to his tribe and to his king. In disputes with the emigrant Boers, who had received sundry rights of grazing from the old king, Sandhlan invariably pitted his memory with complete success against the written and forged documents of the wily Boer farmer. When claims were advanced of palpable mendaciousness Sandhlan soon discovered their weak points and brought his evidence in support of his case with unfailing success. Landmarks and beacons were recalled and indicated, conclusively showing the falsity of the documents produced, and all was done with consummate tact and without strife; for the Swazies always distrusted and feared their powerful Transvaal neighbours. But despite the universal respect with which Sandhlan was regarded by both black and white man, and despite his great age and his personal power and influence, Sandhlan fell. In the words of a letter despatched from the king's kraal by a European trader to the writer at the time (March 1899), describing the incident in witty but caustic vein : ' Sandhlan, after ' serving three kings, got a grand reward, a stroke of rest ' with a knobkerrie. It happened that this " forlorn-' some " philosopher came to know a *leetle* too much for ' his majesty (I beg pardon, HIS MAJESTY), and H.I.M. ' thought fit (and the occasion would never come again) ' to give him a crown of laurels, and in his wrath (I ' mean in his joy) he ordered a wreath and told his ' *shlavelas* (bodyguard) to put it on his head, and by ' some misunderstanding the *shlavelas* took off the ' leaves and brought the bare sticks down with such ' force that he sank under the honour, quite taking away ' his breath. They have tried everything to bring him ' to, but the witch-doctor said it was well done, and they ' have buried him on Execution Kopje. That was all.'

In judging cases of dispute, an induna will seat himself, with his headmen around, whilst the disputants state their case in their turns, standing and gesticulating before the judges. Each has an uninterrupted turn and no question will disturb the harangue. During the hearing the induna will be probably whittling a stick, drinking Kafir beer, or holding a casual conversation, *apropos* of anything, with his neighbour. But in spite of this apparent lack of concern little escapes his attention, and judgment will be delivered without hesitation or conclave, all the quicker, perhaps, because it is generally formed beforehand. An induna in his own particular district will travel about accompanied by a numerous escort, but when he resides at the king's kraal this escort is generally dispensed with; the sun is too near for lesser luminaries to shine. The flattery the induna enjoys at his own kraal he yields to his chief. He becomes a courtier and attends every *indaba* held at the kraal. He has his own special quarters to which repair his own immediate followers from time to time to take his district commands. Another species of induna is he who may be termed the king's favourite. He may not necessarily be of royal kinship or of aristocratic blood. He depends altogether upon the royal favour and never leaves the royal side. He rules more as a parasite than as a constitutional lawmaker. There is frequent jealousy between the two classes.

CHAPTER IV

MISSIONARIES AND NATIVES

MISSION work in South Africa is very difficult. The raw material lies around in abundance, but the ore body is of a recalcitrant nature. After a century of mission work, assisted throughout by the support of the various Governments and facilitated by the religious tendency so marked in the early Dutch, Huguenot, and British settlers, it may not be said that even in the earlier inhabited portion of South Africa the natives in the mass have been converted. Missions have been established for many years not only at the Cape, but as far north as the Zambesi, across the Zambesi in Barotseland, and in Zululand, Basutoland, and Swaziland, yet with one or two exceptions the tribes as a whole have remained in their pristine savagery, receiving the missionary with kindly welcome, attending his teaching in a desultory manner, appreciating his goodness or his great knowledge, but in most cases retaining or reverting to their ancient mode of thought or non-thought. One might hazard the opinion that it is easier to convert a Buddhist, a Mahommedan, a Catholic, or a Protestant from his native religion than a raw Kafir, and for this reason. In the former cases there is ground to go on, there is dogma to attack, there is trained reason to apprehend; but in the case of the Kafir you have to make your soil before you can plant the seed, and when you plant your seed you have no certainty as to growth, which brings you back to the soil again. A raw, amiable, laughing, superstitious native will agree to anything a white man tells him. He will neither argue, question, think, nor take to heart. He will accept everything with blind confidence, and then depart and rejoin his heathen rites. It is only natural that missions have taken some effect. Native Christians are found in all South African communities. But there is no Christian tribe converted by missionaries. The Bechuanas under Khama, due to the memory of Livingstone and the efforts of Dr. Moffat, are the nearest approach to this ideal; but even Khama rules over a mixed horde, and is the only responsible chief in South Africa who has steadfastly embraced the Christian religion. In the early days of Swaziland there were two mission stations, established for years in the land. The missionaries were well housed and comfortably off; but mission 'boys' were scarce. It was popularly reported in those parts among Europeans that when the Bishop made his rounds of inspection the practice was for these missions to borrow converts from their neighbour. This resulted in the Bishop praying with the same little congregation wherever he journeyed, all the while thinking how nicely the work was going on. But even with the aid of this stratagem the assembly was always exceedingly small, as may be vouched for. A larger measure of success has been achieved in other parts, but the net result is not encouraging enough to predict an early acceptance of Christianity by the native, in the proper sense of the word. This disappointing result has been noted by the Rev. Herbert Kelly in the course of a visit to missions in South Africa. He says in a general sense that the activity of the parson and his workers is concentrated far too much upon Church-going, Sunday schools, and other results directly connected with his own machinery, far too little addressed to the building up of an independent religious and Church character. The result appears in the manufacture of Church-goers rather than Churchmen. It seemed to him that precisely this same defect was at work in the mission field. ' If it is true, terribly true, ' that we are doing too little, in another sense, equally ' true, we are doing too much. And if so, it will result ' that we are making mission-boys rather than Chris-' tians.'

In this conclusion Mr. Kelly cleverly hits the mark. The proportion of real Christians to professed Christians among Europeans it is difficult to estimate—judged by human conduct it cannot be large. Among natives the higher-grade are so few that they are numerically lost in the millions of their colour, and it is all the fault of the topsy-turvy system in practice. The missionary will sow the seed before the ground has been properly prepared. Perhaps it would not be so incorrect to say that between wars and missions the Red Indian has all but disappeared. If the past method of converting the heathen in South Africa is retained, the natives of that region will also be in danger. For a further elaboration of this thought we must again turn to the Rev. Mr. Kelly. He says, ' To my mind it seems clear that, ' as a general rule, the native never can, and never does, ' accept Christianity pure from a white man. It is ' always to him mixed with a sense of Europeanisation, ' of " white man's magic," of white protection, however

' hard the missionary may try to disabuse him of that
' view. Of course, there are always exceptional men
' who are capable of seeing the abstract point, and of
' mentally stripping it of the form in which it came to
' them ; but I could give only too many instances where,
' when the white teacher was withdrawn from his work,
' sometimes only temporarily, sometimes in spite of the
' substitution of a native priest, everything forthwith
' fell down flat and had to be rebuilt. This surely is the
' test of the whole business. Of course, there are also
' instances to the contrary, generally where some such
' men as I have described were found to rise to the
' emergency ; but this is only a proof of the rule. What
' we want is a system which shall normally produce that
   result, and be built on it, not one which may be often
' saved by it as a fortunate accident. I put the question
' to the most intelligent native clergy I met, " If we were
' " withdrawn to-morrow, would the Church go on ? "
' " No." " Then," I said, " you are still dependent on the
' " European, not on God." ' But really it is idleness
that is obstructing the growth of true Christianity. Mr.
Kelly sees this in the special case of mission work, for
he says, ' My point is that the whole work should have
' been native from almost the very start. Let them build
' their own church, if not of mud, at least of sun-dried
' bricks, made, laid, and thatched by themselves ; provide
' their own vestments and ornaments from such things
' they have; maintain their own pastor, one of themselves.
' They will know then what they are doing, and can be
' asked to work for an end they can see. It may be, of
' course, impossible to carry out such a plan in its ful-
' ness, the Christian congregation may need a little help
' at starting if they are very few. If they work really

' well we may reward them with a few gifts from England
' in vestments or fittings in which they may take a pride ;
' but this is a very different thing from allowing them to
' suppose that a mysterious Providence has allotted to
' the " meesion " the duty of producing churches as the
' cloud does water and the earth mealies.'

Just as Mr. Kelly arrives at this conclusion in the
special sense of missionary effort, so does Bishop Gaul, of
Mashonaland, apply the same principle in a general sense
to natives. In a communication on the labour question
he said : [1] ' All around us are millions of human beings in
' about the same condition in which our ancestors were
' two thousand years ago, with practically no history,
' few present wants, no forethought, and therefore no
' future. It is ours to give them all that is wanting, to
' train their minds to think, their wills to serve, and
' their moral faculties to appreciate duty.

> Self-reverence, self-knowledge, self-control,
> These three alone lead life to sovereign power.

' I hold that, in the natural order of things, necessity
' comes before choice; " must " comes before ought,
' and work for a living before work for a liking. And,
' as I hold that some sort of work is the heritage of all,
' from the king to the cottager, from the palace to the
' kraal, since life means movement with a purpose, it
' follows that, if we are to do our duty to the native
' races of the countries Providence has given us, they
' must be taught the necessity of work with body and
' brains. . . . The problem before us, therefore, is to
' create such conditions and such wants as shall induce
' a natural (not a fictitious or tyrannical) necessity —
' such a necessity, in fact, as shall practically force every

[1] April 1901.

' able-bodied lad and man in the country to earn his
' own living and the living of his family.'

The gospel of work, we hold, must precede, or at least
run parallel with, the gospel of religion. Daily labour,
civilised habit, trousers and familiarity with the civil
laws prepare the ground for the seed. To our mind a
more useful purpose is served for missionary work to
occupy itself in the towns and centres of industry than
in the interior, and those who may elect to reach the
raw masses in their pristine savagery should devote
attention primarily to inculcate industry and secondarily
to instil religion. Mould your article to proper shape
before inscribing the finishing touches, else the fine
lines become blurred and obliterated in the subsequent
moulding. As the venerable Archdeacon Upscher said,
addressing a mission meeting at Heversham Grammar
School, Westmoreland, 'It only remained to get the
' natives civilised, and to let them live no longer by
' their own impulses and passions. At present, if one
' man hated another he simply waited behind a tree
' or something of that description and when his enemy
' goes past hits him with a knobkerrie, or stabs him
' with an assegai. They tried to teach them to live and
' act by right principles, but their great object was not
' only to instil right principles but to get them to
' understand the principles of work and the dignity of
' labour. *Taking them generally the natives were very*
' *lazy, and as a rule the women did all the work.* The
' man would perhaps do a little now and again, and smoke
' his pipe. They wanted the power to make the natives
' work. . . . They wanted to teach the natives that they
' had a soul as well as a body. They wanted to teach
' them these things and others, and they wanted help to

' teach them those different truths, so that they might be
' happy, and not be a source of danger to the society in
' which they lived.' Archdeacon Upscher speaks with all
the authority of many years of self-sacrificing work
among the aborigines of Africa, persisted in despite many
temptations of spheres with more refined surroundings.
Bishop Hartzell, of the American Methodist Episcopal
Church of Africa, having under his care large and successful missions in Liberia and Rhodesia, in a report
on African work published in the *Sun* of New York,
said on the native question : ' The one overshadowing
' problem . . . is the native problem. The great
' question is how to reduce to the minimum mistakes
' in administration, in the enormously difficult work of
' establishing law and order where for tens of centuries
' government had been but another name for brute force
' . . . The time had come in the providence of God
' when the world needs Africa, and the native African is
' to have his chance under the government of European
' nations. He has held that continent for thousands of
' years. In all that time there has come out of it no
' literature or art or science or written language. Among
' the native millions of central and southern Africa a
' new epoch dawns. I believe that native Africans are
' to have a great future, beginning under the government
' of white nations. In the establishing of law and order
' there must be justice, and the necessary sorrows which
' are incident to the uplifting of a race from barbarism
' to civilisation must be reduced to the minimum.
' Whether in the future there are to be great black
' nationalities I do not know. What I do know, how-
' ever, is that for ages the millions of central and southern
' Africa have not developed a civilisation, and that to-

' day God has placed the responsibilities of their com-
' mercial, intellectual, and spiritual tutelage in the hands
' of European nations. . . *This native question is a far
' greater and more difficult one than can be realised by
' those who have not stood face to face with it.*'

The last pronouncement, italicised advisedly, might
well be taken to heart by those philanthropic bodies in
England who seek from ridiculously inadequate scraps
of information to piece together a theory of native
treatment. It is curious in the governing of such an
Empire as ours what power of detachment is daily
exhibited by the classes. The burning question of
Army reform, the growing burden of taxation, and the
necessity of fiscal reform, one would imagine, in these
days, would be the supreme considerations before the
minds of all ; or the national need for an educational
system acceptable and applicable to all sects and
political divisions. Yet, despite these and other great
questions of supreme importance demanding attention,
time and men of value are found to worry over distant
problems which can in no sense have direct influence or
effect upon the man in the street or the average citizen.
One would imagine that the suggestion or the prospect
of employing African natives in the mines were a
matter purely of local significance, and of adjustment
between the British and, we hope, *civilised* Governments of the regions in question. Yet it is quite plain
that any person holding this common-sense view would
be greatly mistaken.

He would discover upon inquiry that the employment
of natives from Central Africa in the mines of the Rand
is the most particular business of the many religious
societies, and sundry members of Parliament, and of the

democratic labour unions of Great Britain. Colonials, we would be told, are not to be trusted with affairs which so closely affect them. The Catholics alone among the religious sects appear to have sense enough to leave the question in the hands of their numerous and effective colonial missions in Africa, deciding that, if protest is called for, it will be forthcoming from the colonial minister of religion or aroused by the democratic spirit so prominent in colonial thought. The very frail thread of connection which unites the British demonstrators with the subject at all is simply the matter of a contribution to the funds of the missionary societies. If they had the true welfare of the native at heart they would gladly welcome any movement for incorporation of the Hamitic races with the economy and the civilisation of the European. Outside spells tutelage and barbarism ; co-operation spells advancement and survival. It is like keeping an adult in short frocks and feeding him on infant's food in order to maintain his simplicity of thought and action. It is irritating for South Africans to see themselves and their requirements continually under examination ; the circumstance brings the one consolation that they and their doings are deemed of such supreme importance that the British world marches to the conference.

As may be gathered by the excerpts given of African missionary utterances, the popular impression among missionary circles at home, that the native is badly treated and that the colonist requires the British voice to keep him from doing injustice and oppressing his black neighbours, is not the opinion of the missionary class in South Africa. Missionaries are found here and there who give colour to the impression that natives

are enslaved and require protection ; they are the
extremists of their class, just as another section are
in perfect accord with the principle so widely held in
the colonies that the natives must be forced to work by
taxes or other coercing measures ; but the bulk of the
resident missionaries take the broad and sensible view
of the moderate thinker, and though naturally influenced
by the aims they profess, of preaching religion to the
black masses, they recognise more or less unreservedly
that the reigning conditions in South and Central
Africa demand the labour of the native for the native's
own good as well as for the benefit of the European
who is governing and developing the land. The most
successful missions carry this view into practice by
building round them not only congregations of
worshippers, but also centres of industry. Naturally
they prefer that the natives shall work within their own
sphere of influence and retain connection with the
mission ; but if the principle of work is to be carried
to its logical conclusion, then just as the natives are
taught to labour in the exotic atmosphere of missionary
workshops, so should they be encouraged to go afield and
work in the established centres of European enterprise.
Labour is not an artificial plant to be cherished and
subsidised, but a real and daily factor to be incorporated in the daily lives of the converts or the
potential converts.

As a commentary upon the present system adopted
by the missions, which contemplates the native convert
and worker in the narrow sense as a member of the
particular religious community, and not as a brand
snatched from the fire of savagery and contributed to the
world of universal industry, is the demand of H. C. C.

Matiwane, Secretary, Native Congress, in a letter to the editor of the *Natal Mercury*. After demanding in reasonable and respectful terms that the natives have the right of representation in the Natal legislative chambers, he advocates the separation of the mission grant for church and school purposes from the lands devoted to native settlements. He charges the missionaries with dealing arbitrarily with their native converts, in that they dare not build a decent house for fear of being turned off, more particularly should they refrain from joining the Church or attending Communion. He affected to speak for those educated natives who had raised themselves from the common herd by adopting the Christian faith and principles. At the Congress which was held by these people the heathen chiefs were invited. This yields the first spark of independence of action and thought, and shows the fruitlessness of missions in the colonies and of the Aborigines' Society at home striving to obstruct natural evolution and endeavouring to place a ring fence around a native community to keep them from contact with the industrial centres and more particularly from the mining industry —the greatest civilising factor in the land, with all its temptations, pitfalls, and rough experiences. The drift of this discourse of Matiwane's shows that as soon as a permanent effect is made upon the black masses by the missionary, absolute independence of the dictation of the Mother Church will be demanded, and the converted will revert to the body politic, discarding all leading-strings and artificial barriers.

This danger has already received official attention. In the course of the proceedings at the Customs Union Conference held at Bloemfontein last March, Mr.

Payne, M.L.A., one of the Natal delegates, moved a resolution to the effect ' (1) That this Conference regards with considerable concern the propagation among the native population of the tenets of what is known as the Ethiopian Church, and expresses the opinion that concerted action with reference thereto should be taken by the Governments of the various Colonies of South Africa. (2) That the clergymen of the Church should not be licensed as marriage officers, or in any way recognised. (3) That continued effort be made to suppress the alleged propaganda of dangerous political and treasonable teaching which is undoubtedly unsettling the native mind.' This resolution, however, together with an amendment against appointing native marriage officers or recognising native clergymen not under the control of a white Church, was eventually withdrawn by leave of the Conference, the members doubtless concluding that such sweeping restrictions were premature before a full consideration of the Native Problem. At a meeting in connection with Church work held in the Hoare Memorial Hall of the Church House, St. Peter's, Eaton Square, Lord Nelson presiding, Rev. F. W. Puller— quoting the *Times* report—gave an interesting account of the history and present position of the Ethiopian movement. It originated eleven years ago with a knot of Wesleyan natives at Johannesburg, who were prevented from exercising their evangelistic gifts by the Wesleyan authorities, and who, therefore, separated and formed a new and exclusively native ' Ethiopian Church.' Two years later they obtained a leader in a distinguished native minister who had also seceded from the Wesleyans. This leader was made a 'Bishop' by the presiding Bishop of the African Methodist Episcopal Church from the United States, but his action was disowned by the other Bishops of that body. The Ethiopians, their leader having come in contact with the Anglican rector of Queenstown and asked his advice, broke with the Americans and petitioned the Bishops in South Africa for a valid episcopate and priesthood. The Bishops had drawn up a scheme for an Ethiopian order within the Church, as desired by the petitioners, and had intimated that they might perhaps have a special Bishop at some future time. Many of their ex-ministers, already well grounded in the Bible, had now been or were being trained for ordination, and by this time at least 1,000 of the community had been confirmed. The total would probably reach 5,000. These people took their religion tremendously in earnest; and they were exceedingly liberal. It was necessary to say, however, that there were other bodies calling themselves Ethiopians, including seceders from the Baptists and Presbyterians, and some who still remained in connection with the African Methodist Episcopal Church. The Archbishop of Cape Town said that the South African Bishops had given information as to their action in this Ethiopian matter to the late and present Archbishops of Canterbury, who had declared that the problem was being solved in the wisest way.

In the excellent autobiography by Mr. Roger Pocock, entitled 'A Frontiersman' (Methuen & Co.), recently published, missionary work is well and kindly though not too hopefully referred to. 'People,' says Mr. Pocock, ' often ask if missions are any good—I ' think ungenerously. The work is always disheartening,

' not from wickedness in the teacher so much as from
' total failure of the savage. We cannot raise him all of
' a sudden to the plane which we have reached through
' many centuries of upward growth. He never attains
' the status of our manhood, the base on which rests our
' Christianity ; and our religion yields but a sickly crop
' outside the boundaries of the Caucasian field. Mean-
' while the missionary—a good man—and his wife, more
' useful than himself, preserve the savage from death by
' contact with our civilisation, teach him all he can
' learn, heal his sickness, comfort him in trouble, and
' keep him out of mischief when otherwise he would be
' out on the warpath scalping our scattered laity. Even
' with no conversions a year, the missionary—loneliest
' of pioneers, remotest of frontiersmen—is a living
' protest to Heaven that we whites are not wholly
' ruthless towards the weaker brethren. If our gifts to
' the heathens were limited to trade guns, gin, and fancy
' disease, not one of us would be able when the time
' came to end up or die without the most horrid
' apprehensions. But with ever so little love the work
' tells.'

That the missionary does good may not be gain-
said. He does good where he educates and where he
spreads the gospel of industrial efficiency. But the
thousands of pounds yearly contributed to missionary
funds may scarcely be deemed as given by the donors
for secular education or for the eradication of laziness among the natives. The incentive is the spread
of the holy gospel, and by these fruits should the
missionary be tested. It is a matter of considerable
satisfaction to the colonist that missionary efforts find
on the whole greater vent, and achieve more utility

and success, in the schooling and training of their flock than in propagating a religious teaching which in the nature of the material can only be skin deep. We do not imply by this that the colonist is averse from spreading the gospel among the natives, and lifting their thoughts and their ethics to a more spiritual plane; but that he knows while the mass of native mankind remains imbedded in the clay of laziness, irresponsibility, and savagery, all the surface polish of Church teaching serves little purpose, while industry and secular education bare the soul. As we know, most professing Christians among Europeans fail to live up to their belief. The many fall very short; the few just see the promised land. The natives in their present stage of development are much more heavily handicapped in their endeavours. Rooted in centuries of savage rites, the soil itself must be treated and changed ere due effect may be hoped for in the fruit.

CHAPTER V

'EXETER HALL' AND ITS INFLUENCE

NEXT to that of Mr. Gladstone, perhaps, the name which arouses the spleen of the average colonist in South Africa most is 'Exeter Hall.' Not that the grand qualities of the one past factor and the excellent intentions of the other influence on South African affairs are not appreciated at their proper worth. All homage is rendered by the liberty-loving colonial to the great Liberal statesman for his love of freedom and of political rectitude, and due credit is given to such as Sir Charles Dilke and other prominent ladies and gentlemen for the well-meaning interest they take in the aborigines. But just as the nether regions are said to be paved with good intentions, so have the honest endeavours of these good people caused a vast amount of ill-blood in South Africa. To Mr. Gladstone's weakness may be traced the responsibility of the injustice done to Transvaal Britishers at the period of the first war, and a great portion of responsibility for the blood spilt in the second war. Theoretically in London the principles of the Aborigines' Society are sound and praiseworthy : when brought into practice in South Africa they become impracticable and productive of strife. Doubtless the votaries of aborigines' protection will ascribe the irritation their sayings and doings

arouse in the colonial mind to the circumstance that
the unholy and cruel colonist would subject the races
over which he rules to slavery, torture, and other
severities, and is only checked in his cruelty and greed
for slave labour by the philanthropical representations
of the Society. It certainly does appear, according to
the lucubrations which issue from its secretary, that
there are no well-wishers among European colonists
towards their black fellow-citizens. In his eyes the
Governments of the pioneer and mining communities
are banded together in one wicked league to oppress
the native, who has only the Aborigines' Society to look
to for protection. This Society does not move on the
lines of such cognate institutions as that, for instance, for
the Prevention of Cruelty to Animals, or to Children,
confining itself, as do they, to specific transgressions and
stated cases ; the method adopted is the very convenient
one of general condemnation, with the British Cabinet
to act as the agent of inquiry. Instead of basing their
actions on the common-sense view that the Europeans
in South Africa are just as kindly inclined as their
brothers at home, and must be considered a greater
authority on a subject with which they are familiar
than others some 6,000 miles distant, the unwarranted
assumption is held that the stay-at-homes are better
fitted to weigh local conditions governing the treatment
of natives than the residents themselves. Though the
Society's representations are received with courtesy by
the British Government in office, and its attacks on
Imperial and Colonial administration welcomed by the
Opposition for the time being, Colonial Ministers,
while respecting their social and political influence,
evade the practice of their teaching. Mr. Chamber-

lain, while he received their deputations with proper courtesy, and academically approved of their pious aims, reserved his real conclusions on the root matter.

Very characteristic of the broad statements with no pith in which the Aborigines' Society delights to indulge is a statement which appeared some time ago in a publication called 'The Aborigine's Friend.' In enumerating outlying questions it was asserted that ' in Rhodesia the demands for imported and forced ' labour, and the plans for supplying these demands, are ' assuming more and more alarming shapes.' The casual reader perusing this—which had no context or other reference to the subject—would assume, and with very good reason, that the natives in Rhodesia, already in an abject and fearsome condition, were about to be manacled and sent in batches to the mines and farms of the Europeans. Yet the actual condition was almost ludicrously different. While the Aborigines' Society was filling its adherents, and trying to imbue the Government and the public, with dire tidings of native slavery, the residents, at their wits' end for labour, were memorialising their Government to initiate some measure in order to induce the native to offer his labour for a liberal wage! One must conclude by the peculiar and often outrageous statements circulated by the Aborigines' Society that they are based merely upon the irresponsible reports of some second-rate authority. The Society has no recognisable agent in South Africa, not to mention an official one. The natives themselves as a mass are sublimely ignorant of its existence, and the Society does not advance the pretence that it represents native thought.

Dismissing from consideration the personal aspect

of the case—whether the Aborigines' Protection Society
is properly equipped or otherwise to pose as arbiter
of the fate of the natives and attitudinise as censor of
colonial morals—the native question in South Africa is
so closely bound with its political, social, and industrial
life that what a small sect in England consider a
matter of mild employment and a subject for amiable
endeavour is a problem of the deepest importance to
the communities in the colonies.   It is the one burning
question which, if handled without prudence and
moderation by the Imperial Government, will unite
Briton and Boer, Administrator and people, against
the interloping outsider.

As giving weight and authority to these warnings
to-day one may refer to Mr. McCall Theal's ' Progress
of South Africa in the Century,' graphically illustrating
the dire effects in the past of this mischievous interference.   The history of South Africa shows innumerable
conflicts and occasions for dissatisfaction, leading to
trouble, in the attempt to legislate for the native from
the home ideal and ignoring colonial sentiment.   The
London Missionary Society preached ' the absolute
equality of men of all races.'   In 1811, owing to the
representation of the directors of the society, inspired
by a Rev. Mr. Read, an impeachment of the colonists
was framed.   Mr. Read, aided by other members of his
society, coached the cases before the circuit court.   Over
fifty-eight colonists, mainly of Dutch extraction, had to
stand their trial.   The whole country was in a state of
commotion, and 1,000 witnesses, European, black, and
Hottentot, were summoned to give evidence.   Yet, after
a four months' session, and extraordinary means used
by the Government and the missionaries to bring the

alleged malefactors to justice, with the court consisting
of two judges and no jury, the greater number of cases
were proved to be without foundation, and the characters
of the Governor, the Landdrost, and the colonists were
cleared. It was these events which materially contributed to the dissatisfaction so often expressed, and
resulted in the exodus of the Boers from British rule.
Surrounded by hordes of savages, they were convinced
that the policy of the Government was to make life
a burden to them by favouring native idleness, native
theft, and native rule. As described by Mr. McCall
Theal: ' The London Missionary Society occupied in
' South Africa a position different from all the others.
' It had not only a greater number of agents, but its
' openly avowed principles brought it into conflict with
' the Government and the colonists, and created an
' antagonism towards it that has not even yet wholly
' died out. Its superintendents put themselves in
' the position of advocates for the coloured people,
' and brought innumerable complaints before the direc-
' tors of the society in England instead of before the
' Government in Capetown, thus drawing upon them-
' selves the hostility of the local authorities. In their
' view it was oppression to make a distinction in any way
' between coloured people and Europeans, and through
' their publications they caused the colonists to be
' regarded abroad as unjust and cruel because Hottentot
' and negro servants were not treated as equals socially.
' Several of the most prominent among them, notably
' Dr. Vanderkemp, their first superintendent, put their
' principles into practice by marrying coloured women,
' and their processions were usually led by a white and
' a negro child carrying a banner with the motto, *Ex*

' *uno sanguine*. Dr. Philip, the second superintendent,
' maintained that he knew an educated Bushman—
' whom, however, no one else had ever seen—intel-
' lectually equal to a European. It was not a question
' of religion, but a question whether a barbarian could at
' one bound attain the top rung of the ladder to which
' Europeans have climbed slowly and painfully through
' countless generations, that divided the colonists from
' the London Missionary Society.'

The practice and results of the London Missionary
Society's interference were eminently exemplified in the
career of the Rev. Dr. Philip, the second superintendent,
a man of great bodily vigour and natural ability and
utterly fearless. He was not over-scrupulous as to
means in gaining his ends, and the successive governors
regarded him as a dangerous factor in society. In the
Kafir Wars of 1835 this Dr. Philip was a bitter
opponent of the Governor, Sir Benjamin D'Urban, who
arrived in the colony in complete sympathy with the
views of the home philanthropic societies, but under-
went a change in his opinions on closer acquaintance-
ship with the existing conditions. While the Scotch
Wesleyan missionaries supported the Governor in his
endeavour to persuade the natives to become British
subjects, Dr. Philip fought determinedly against the
policy. He travelled to England accompanied by a
Kafir and a Hottentot trained in his schools, and was
warmly received by the missionary and philanthropic
societies at home. This resulted in Lord Glenelg, the
Secretary of State for the Colonies, undoing all Sir
Benjamin D'Urban's actions, and taking his cue from
Dr. Philip and his Society against the expressed wishes
of the legislative council, the colonists, English and

Dutch alike, and nearly all the local missionaries of other denominations. Everything was abandoned, and, according to the historian, ' the condition of affairs on the Kafir border was thrown back to what it had been twenty years before.' Naturally the blood shed in the wars with Mosilekatse and Dingaan sorely grieved Dr. Philip ; he grieved for the poor natives and not for the murdered Boers. Consequently by his recommendation, supported by the missionary societies at home, a number of independent native states were marked out, with the inevitable result that a series of devastating wars followed. In the end, in 1846, Sir Harry Smith, after years of past bloody warfare, had to revert to the policy of Sir Benjamin D'Urban, so stoutly resisted by Dr. Philip and traversed by Lord Glenelg. Dr. Philip subsequently saw the error of his ways and raised no objection to this reversion of policy. In the words of the historian, ' The Rev. Dr. Philip had seen his plans ' terminate in disaster, and when Jan Tshatshu, whom ' he had exhibited in England as a Christian Kafir, took ' part in the atrocities with which the war commenced, ' he became a changed man . . . . when Tshatshu's ' defection was announced he broke down completely. ' Soon afterwards he retired to the mission station, ' Hankey, and never again took part in politics.'

The story of Dr. Philip, as gleaned from this veracious history, points a great moral and adorns a modern tale. Will it be taken to heart by our modern Colonial Secretaries ? The position assumed in earlier times by the London Missionary Society is now occupied by the Aborigines' Protection Society.

CHAPTER VI

NATIVES AND INDUSTRY

As those who have followed us so far will have seen, we pin our faith upon real, inculcated, and, if necessary, coercionary measures to induce labour among the natives as the first and most essential steps to their ethical and mental advancement. The coloured population of Africa deserve on the whole a kindly consideration from their more favoured white master ; for, disguise it as we may, master and servant it is, and not the brotherly relation of which so much is heard on religious and philanthropic platforms. The principle advocated by the colonists is to induce the necessity of labour, in order to provide the native with means to dress and live decently, and prepare the ground for those higher ethical and spiritual teachings, so popularly associated with proper clothing and civilised habits of life. The young of these Europeanised natives, accustomed to labour and clothing, take more naturally to European teaching. Most enthusiasts for native progress go astray in their unfortunate obliquity of vision, failing to appreciate that the only proper and practical method of assisting and raising the native is by working in unison with the European employers of labour; looking after the native's spiritual and educational needs while the employer is teaching the dignity of labour. If the two races are to live peaceably side by side both must work for a living, and the burden of improving the land and providing revenue must not rest solely on the shoulders of the heavily taxed European. There is no question of native slavery or enforcing any particular kind of labour. The proper solution is by a judicious application of laws tending to lead the native into an industrious from an idle life, and raise him to that higher plane of civilisation where Christian teaching may be safely grafted upon industry.

The colonist deeply resents the attempts to obstruct periodically ordered by the irresponsibles in England with the motive of checking local efforts to solve the native problem. The underlying principle of the colonists' demand for measures to coerce the natives into providing that labour which their numbers reasonably allow is based upon the law which obtains at home against vagrancy. The native is neither farmer, agriculturist, nor grazier proper, yet he lives on and by the land. In years of plenty he revels in inordinate feeding and drinking; in years of famine he either dies or receives Government assistance. In either event he idles half the year. As bearing upon this contention, quite recently Mr. Knight, the well-known correspondent of the *Morning Post*, in passing through Linchwe's country, remarked : ' Linchwe, the ' paramount chief of the country to which we were now ' travelling, shrewdly taking action in anticipation of the ' days of dearth, has compelled a large proportion of his ' young men to leave his kraals and seek work at once. ' Were it left to them they would, with the usual native ' improvidence, postpone the taking of this step until

' the last moment; that is, until after they had spent
' all the money they had made during the war, had ex-
' hausted their stores of grain, and had starvation at
' the door.'

In former days, under the rule of their savage chiefs,
the superfluous energy of the younger men was directed
to raiding the weaker tribes, the latter class having perforce to work the year through to provide their own
elementary needs in addition to the loot carried away
by their oppressors. Under civilised conditions the *rôles*
of both erstwhile oppressor and oppressed are identical. They neither raid nor are raided, but have to
till or cause their women to till for immediate needs,
idling the rest of their time away, and providing very
little, if any, reserve. This idleness of the rank and
file works disastrously on themselves and on their
fellow-citizens the Europeans. Industry is a necessity
to civilised life, and the greater the industry the higher
the civilisation. Industry demands good government,
and good government entails taxes. Owing to the wild
and idle life of the native his needs and ambitions are
few; the taxes he pays are therefore infinitesimal. Idleness tends to mischief, crime, and immorality. The
Draconian laws of the chiefs are suspended and the mild
rule of the European gives not only liberty but allows of
considerable license. This reacts unfavourably on the
tribesmen themselves, and necessitates special police
and laws of self-protection and preservation. Upon the
European falls the main burden of taxation, and the
natives enjoy the best fruits of the expenditure. Having
this in view, the exasperation of the colonist can be
well imagined when he is forced to go far afield for
labour while the material he seeks lolls on his doorsteps

and partakes of his fruits of industry. This is intensified
when, after a year's drought and visitation of locusts,
the additional burden of sustenance of life is added to
the normal one of paying for native administration.

The colonist simply demands that the native
section of the community, instead of leading a life of
sloth and irresponsibility, shall be made to work in the
vocation the individual may select, granting him a wage
which provides not only the means of procuring the
necessaries of life but also its luxuries. The prevailing
rate of native pay in South Africa in all but rare cases
includes board, lodging, and medical attendance. The
hours of labour at the mines are less than those in
vogue at home, and afterwards the native worker's
movements are perfectly free. He enjoys all the
advantages of citizenship short of franchise, which even
the most rabid negrophilist would scarcely advocate to
be given to ignorant savages. He has complete access
to all the avenues of redress the law provides, and
does not hesitate as a rule in summoning his employer
when a grievance troubles him, as the records of the
local Magistrates' Courts can show. His term of
employment is purely voluntary, the most prominent
grievance the employer has to-day being the propensity
of the native to leave his employment on short service
and just when his untutored hands have commenced to
become a little skilled. He has a native department
all to himself in addition to the ordinary advantages
a stable government offers. It is therefore seen that
he receives more than a living wage, his service is
voluntary, he leaves at the expiration of his agreed
term of service—and often deserts before—is protected
by the same law that protects the white man, and has

recourse to it when he deems himself unjustly dealt by. This is South African enforced labour!

Viewing the matter broadly, the prime factor which attaches the native to his home is the racial abhorrence of all hard and sustained labour. Labour has always been regarded as a punishment and a mark of servitude in native polity, with the exception of that sort of work which fits in with his pastoral or nomad life. He will cover miles as a letter-carrier for a small guerdon; cut wood, act as policeman, or undertake any task which lends itself to the enjoyment of occasional dawdling; but to set, resolute, and unfailing labour such as at the mines, with their regular hours and ties on liberty, he presents an uncompromising front. Those who repair to the mines do so under the pressure of lack of substance, of starvation, or of pure love of adventure, of strong spirits or of avarice. Few indeed travel to the mining districts in order to better their social position or improve their mode of living. A native does not aspire to become a mining magnate or a retired storekeeper. Steady and regular work is not an accepted part of his life; it is an ugly episode in his career of ease. To accustom the native to steady work is a task which will take years to accomplish, and while other and more congenial avenues are open to him it is only natural that he will repair to the mines only as a last resource.

Such favourite remedies as taxing him individually and taxing his wives, though tending towards the desired end, fall short of the desired purpose. A native may just as well have one wife and six concubines living with their own people as seven wives living at their husband's kraal. He will either not connect the tax with labour or, if he should, he will look upon labour with added dislike as a penalty, and not as a duty. Going to the root of the problem, the pressure must come from within, and not from without. A higher standard of living must be imported into the kraal, and the native, while at work at the mines, must be educated to higher wants and higher ambitions, so that when he returns to his home his neighbours may regard him with envy, inducing emulation. His wife or wives should be encouraged to dwell with him or visit him during his term of service, so that the female element shall also be imbued with higher views. In brief, the native labourer of natural growth has yet to be evolved from the mixed mass of sable humanity which covers the land from the Cape to Cairo, and no short cut to that end has been discovered.

In a despatch to Mr. Chamberlain on the native question in Rhodesia, dated October 4, 1901, Lord Milner thus diagnosed the character of the native: ' The black man is naturally inclined, much more than ' the white, to do nothing at all. As the economic ' compulsion which is found in European countries does ' not exist here, he will, if left to himself, generally live ' in absolute idleness, without adding in any way to the ' productive power of the country in which he lives. ' I cannot conceive that, under any except the most · distorted code of morals, it can be thought right for ' us to encourage him in this attitude, or even not to ' dissuade him from it by all reasonable means.' Mr. Robert Wallace, Professor of Agriculture and Rural Economy in Edinburgh University, in a paper read by him at the Royal Colonial Institute after a visit to South Africa in March 1901, said : ' The most im-

' portant question at issue in South Africa was that of
' labour. Unless some method were found to induce
' the black man to work, the development of South
' Africa in all but the richest mines would be indefinitely
' postponed. The men, in the full knowledge of, and by
' permission of, the Government of this country, acted
' as lords and masters, and treated their women as their
' slaves, while they remained in indolence, a rapid
' growing menace to the community in general. By
' common consent school education in Great Britain
' was compulsory. This was a distinct interference
' with the liberty of the subject in the undoubted
' interest of the individual, although the average school-
' boy in his ignorance and inexperience held different
' views. It would be an injury to the black population
' to adopt for them an European standard of education,
' but that the black man had a right to the education
' which was best suited to his state of existence no
' one would deny, and that it was the duty of the State to
' provide the means should be patent to every one who
' possessed an enlightened sense of the necessity of
' elevating the lower races that came under our domina-
' tion. It would be a dream of the wildest description
' to attempt to elevate an idle community. Manual
' labour was undoubtedly the form of education which
' black men stood in need of—in their own interests, in
' that of the women who were now forced by them to
' do more than their fair share of work, and in even the
' greater interest of the body politic. A black man
' ought to be as capable as a white of being taught to
' appreciate the dignity of labour, and surely if it were
' good for the one it could not be harmful for the other.'
Even the missionary, who is naturally inclined to

preach leniency in dealing with the native, clearly sees the error in leaving him to his own idle devices.

Father Rickartz, of the Chushawasha Mission of Rhodesia, says : ' If a man did not work he would never ' become a proper Christian, because, according to the ' law of Christ, a man should work, and it was a crime ' and a sin if a man were idle. If the boy did not work, ' if he did not want to work, and if everything was done ' that could be lawfully done to make him work, then it ' was necessary to force him. Parents were, for instance, ' forced to send their children to school ; people in ' civilised nations to become soldiers.' Another missionary of considerable experience and authority among natives, the Rev. J. W. Stanlake of Tegwane, a Wesleyan minister, said in the course of an address given at the annual district synod at Salisbury, addressing a native audience : ' Years ago you were under the ' tyranny of the Matabele. With the white people came ' freedom and peace. In their train came Scriptures and ' missionaries. Vast sums have been spent to raise you ' up. In return you must show your gratitude by ' serving them ; don't be afraid of work. Christianity ' means obedience and service.'

The foregoing applies directly to that great mass of untrained and unskilled humanity to be found in various grades of civilisation, from the naked savage of the trans-Zambesian regions to the semi-clothed Zulu of Natal and Xosas of the Cape Colony. As is natural among a race with such peculiar powers of adaptation, showing no signs of retiring before the flood of European settlement, those tribes which have come into closest and more permanent contact with the European have exhibited many variants from the common rule. For instance, at the seaports a class of native stevedore has evolved, quite accustomed to steady work and a liberal wage. These tend to drift into the ranks of the coloured classes as distinguished from the blacks, where such mixed communities persist, such as at Capetown, Port Elizabeth, and Delagoa Bay. In Natal the Zulus of the ports and the towns retain their racial purity of blood and language much more rigidly. Yet while many become wedded to their new life and calling, a large proportion after a term hie back to their kraals and rejoin the ranks of their origin. Some natives develop into petty traders, while a few become artisans and mechanics, but not sufficient by any means to affect the argument previously set forth in this chapter. The industrial position so peculiar and difficult in South Africa is the presentment at one and the same time of copious means for employment and great quantities of human beings without employment. And the case of the native is that he can rub along with his simple wants very well without employment, or at least with the minimum of employment. He has no incentive to work or ambitions to satisfy, short of a wife or two, which he may obtain for the rest of his natural life by means of putting in twelve months' labour. His land is secured to him in almost every South African State. Native reserves are native preserves given to the black without any such imperative motive as stopping extinction. He shows no signs of extinction, but rather tends to overcrowd. In former days such conditions were met by recourse to slavery; utilising the ignorant and fallow material basking in the sun without care or thought, and relieving the native from the burden of his undiluted environment with its concomitant of wars and slaughter. South Africa, as it is to-day, has been created by the European, with the hired service of as many of the blacks as could be persuaded to work ; for even the old Dutch slaves were not a numerous class compared with the population from which they were drawn. No Bantu tribe has developed a land with any design to emulate its neighbours. They have looked on with a kind of good-humoured indifference, while the towns of the whites grew beside them, around them, and passed them by. All efforts to protect the natives from work only tend to prolong an impossible situation. There is no parallel in earlier times of a Kimberley, a Johannesburg, or a Bulawayo becoming established amid a stationary savage black race with full license and liberty to remain stationary. In other days the aborigines would either have become forcibly absorbed in the new and the higher order, or been forcibly utilised as slaves. In Africa, great Mahommedan states have been built up from the embers and the ashes of cannibalism and savagery. In ancient Egypt and Carthage the blacks were relegated to the slave pits and bondage. In these enlightened times the Europeans are too proud to permit or encourage absorption or assimilation of race and colour, and too just and merciful to entertain any method of slavery. In North America and Australia the coloured question solved itself through a long course of wars, sale of alcohol, small-pox, and pneumonia. In South Africa measures are taken to forbid any such factor operating to the detriment of the native. If left alone doubtless in the course of years some real impression will be made on native thought and character ; but the world moves rapidly in these times, and industry once impelled on its road brooks no delay. If the mines of the Rand and Rhodesia were to await a native conversion to civilised principles, then thousands of Europeans would suffer in the process; and the modern man suffers with impatience an ill which is anomalous and may be remedied. Hence the pursuit of labour for the Rand.

The indolence of the native is not confined to South Africa, for we find that the German colonies of East and West Africa have the same circumstance to contend with. Mr. Buchanan, Secretary to the British Embassy at Berlin, in his report on the German colonies, remarks that ' all the efforts of the authorities, as well as the ' preaching of the gospel of work by the missionaries, ' have borne but little fruit.' In East Africa, says Mr. Buchanan, ' the wants of the native are so few that it ' is difficult to offer any inducement tempting him to ' make him overcome his natural disinclination to work.' Count Goetzen, the Governor of German East Africa, openly avowed, at a meeting of the Colonial Society at Berlin, that he had experimented in pure compulsion. In reply to some criticism of such methods of modified slavery, he explained the plan adopted : ' I summoned,' he said, ' the headmen of the neighbouring villages, ' and pointed out to them the advantages to be derived ' from planting the surrounding waste lands with oil ' palms, maize, and sugar cane. After lengthy discussions ' with them, I eventually gave orders that each village ' should lay out and plant one field with whatever would ' grow best on it, and that each native in the village ' should work twelve days in the year on it. The pro- ' ceeds of their labour are to be divided in three equal ' shares between the headman, the villagers, and the ' Commune of Dar-es-Salaam, the last-named under-

' taking to send the produce for sale to the coast.' This directness of application is typical of German methods, and there is a great deal to be said in its justification.

All past experiences in South Africa have shown that the native, if left to work out his own salvation under the benign rule of the Britisher, tends to become a drag on the progress of the community rather than a useful portion of the workers. In Natal and the Cape Colony, outside the small proportion of Kafirs employed at the seaports, at the farms, and in domestic service, the natives as a section of the political system are neither material producers nor large consumers. The class which alone becomes valuable and *creative* in both directions of economy consists of those who work at mining. These are essentially the sinews and the labourers of their kind; they are also peculiarly the section which promotes in the raw mass general commerce by new desires—excited by contact with civilisation — for clothing, ornament, and imported food. The ' boy ' who departs from his home to labour at the mines, or other contract work, earns in the course of a few months sufficient coin to pay for the needs of his father, mother, sisters, and brothers for the year, and when he returns at the expiration of his time, often possesses in his well-lined pouch sufficient funds to lay by a nucleus of competency in the purchase of a wife or two and a couple of cows or heifers, living happily ever after on the compound increase of his first earnings. When this pleasant routine is followed by the native labourer he apparently scores, and so do his people; but such is not, fortunately, always the case. Sometimes he becomes enamoured with his new life of trousers and tie ; often he embraces the tenets of Christianity and voluntarily seeks knowledge in School and Mission Church. In Krugerian times of the Transvaal he often fell a victim to drink, and got to love the canteen more than his old home; sometimes he married some sable wench of his own colour, though not of his own tribe; in fact many circumstances arise which often prevail against the homesickness of the absent son or brother. Under these latter circumstances it is the European community of industry and civilisation which benefits together with the emancipated one. Another brand is snatched from the fire of ignorance, savagery, and lazy thraldom. This process of absorption of the black into the social system of the white is, however, disappointingly slow, with not much prospect of being accelerated by time. In the older established South African colonies the natives under the cold and careless rule of colonial law have, to a large extent, become confirmed and stereotyped into their peaceful habits of lethargy, only occasionally broken by fitful efforts to work. This great mass of dormant and dull humanity, increasing in numbers without a corresponding increase in mental advancement, is lying like a nightmare on the imagination of the thinking section of South African colonists. The native problem, growing in intensity, occasionally disturbs the serenity of colonial legislators, but the mere cursory examination of the threatened danger is always enough to dissipate the courage of the reforming statesmen; the problem is shelved for another generation to solve.

Though this dangerous state of native affairs has persisted in the past there is no reason why it should continue in the future. The great bulk of natives are still in their primitive state and ready to take the trend where the guiding hand may lead them. If left to their own devices and allowed full liberty to grow like the lily of the field—or the thistle or any other pretty but useless and clogging weed—they will develop into a social danger, and perhaps become an avalanche which some fear will one day overwhelm the whites. If, on the other hand, they are kindly but firmly led into those avenues of labour and social advancement which are open to them, they will have the chance to take their place in the political and industrial system of the colony, and may live, thrive, and multiply in peace and comfort side by side with their European fellow-citizens. They will occupy the positions to which they are suited, live contented lives, and should they ever develop their mental powers and rise to the same plane as their white neighbours, even then—which is a long time to look forward—they may with some reason hope to assume peaceably the position to which their intellect would entitle them—for the land is big and scope will be found for all. But it is the present and the immediate future to which we must look, and which mostly concern us. The question which South Africans are called to answer is : Are the natives to grow up and multiply as free and licensed weeds in a field of struggling corn, or are they to be trained, tended, and developed into one of the fertilising elements which reinforce and assist the natural growth of progress and prosperity, the fruits of which they themselves will proportionately enjoy? There can scarcely be but one answer to this question. They must be induced to work; for our sake, for theirs, and for the sake of the country. Enlightened colonists would be glad to see the natives advance in morality, civilisation, and in religion, on the same philanthropic —or selfish—grounds as held by the higher classes of England in their desire to give the proletariat educational facilities to raise the mean level of the nation. The fallacy that to keep the nigger of service to his master he must be kept in mental and political subjection is on a par with the argument often heard at home that since the Board Schools have been established the lower classes have deteriorated in usefulness. The true native policy is to steadily raise the level of the native by precept and by active government practice, and the first medium to this result should be steady pressure upon him to work and honestly accept the new conditions reigning in the land. If the plaints of such bodies of mischievous people as are banded together at home to obstruct the industrial progress of the blacks be heeded, then not only will a disservice be rendered to the unconscious *protégés* themselves, but also to the land and the pioneer people living there. The policy should be to stir the natives to activity in such spheres as mining, agriculture, and in general industrial employment. Hand in hand with this paternal discipline, such other media should be employed as simple and inexpensive channels for education, and the encouragement of approved missions, teaching that the dignity of labour is one of the essences of true religion. Ministers and schools that foolishly and mischievously train the young native to consider himself an equal in every respect of the European should be courageously discouraged, even forbidden. The natives of South Africa as a race are not, nor will be for years, or generations, the

intellectual rivals to the European, even should they
ever become so. The sole equality between the two
elements consists in physical form and strength, and it
is even doubtful if these obtain. There are exceptions
here as elsewhere. Some natives have distinguished
themselves from their fellows in their capacity to learn
and absorb real civilised thought and action, though
not one has, as yet, in South Africa, reached any considerable eminence in literature, commerce, or politics.
Those that cross the high barrier have certain facilities
to enable them to achieve, though obviously somewhat
handicapped by their colour. Yet colour alone is no
insuperable disqualification. Despite a few isolated
cases the mass of the blacks remain in their backward
condition, and it is to the interest of both white and
black that, subject to an avoidance of any undue or
inflated status being thrust upon them, the natives be
guided into their proper vocations and educated up to
their future level in the bodies politic and economic,
so that they live at present, and continue to progress
in the future, side by side and amicably with their
superior and better equipped fellow-citizens of European
extraction, without embarrassment to themselves or
to their white masters, teachers, and well-intentioned
friends.

CHAPTER VII

THE PROBLEM

WITH some five or six million natives in the land in various stages of evolution; sentient, robust, and not to be denied; calmly awaiting the period of their emancipation from the trammels of barbarism; not too eager to learn, disinclined for work, yet on the whole tractable and expectant, what policy should be adopted by the European to utilise this strength without exhausting it, to raise the native from his present low level without swamping the superior caste? This is the problem to be solved; a problem unsolved in the past, no nearer solution in the present, and looming threateningly in the future. Two half-expressed ideals stand out clearly in the treatment of this dark mass of 'child-like' humanity. One section of colonial thought would adopt a passive and cautious policy, a policy of fear of arousing the indifferent and slumbering giant; another, bolder in thought and more anticipatory in action, would tackle the problem in its present malleable state, and direct the forces at the outset to the channels by which they may flow safely to their ultimate goal. The latter and bolder course is that of admitting cautiously the current of native intellectual and industrial development to the broad and permanent stream of European civilisation; the

advocates of a more timid and opportunist policy
would retain the barriers of colour and caste rigidly
and absolutely and deprive the current of native progress of its proper egress to the broad river of safety,
until, perchance, the accumulated 'sudd' become arbitrarily and forcibly pierced and the waters overwhelm
the surrounding country. There are arguments for
both sides, but we would recommend the bolder course.

The general feeling of prejudice against education
and mechanical skill in the native, so pronounced in
South African colonists of the up-country type, is not
so much a reflection of narrow minds as it is a sign of
protest against a policy of 'coddling' and artificially
raising the native in the human scale. In common
with the great bulk of the colonial community, we
have the same condemnation of those missionaries
and others who would preach equality where no equality
exists, and who deem it their duty to train the raw
native in an artificial atmosphere at mission stations,
where workshops and all necessaries and a good many
luxuries of life are provided which cannot be found
outside these locations for his class. But it is quite
compatible whilst holding these views to hold that
where the native can be raised from his present low
plane in the industrial scale by the judicious establishment of Government schools, pure and simple, without
segregating him from his own sphere in the industrial
world, offering a medium to those who desire to raise
their intellectual standard and sharpen their wits and
increase their industry, such a policy is conducive of
good to black and white alike, and tends to industrial,
commercial, and social betterment. History can produce no community which has ultimately gained by

keeping the lower classes in ignorance, and it is most exceptional—if a case be found—where higher education has proved truly detrimental to the public weal. We hold that this thesis applies to a mixed community as to a single race, and that the sense of fear of native rivalry in trade and politics is only another phase of the Krugerian Uitlander repressive doctrine recently exploded with such force. Whatever the nature of the problem to be solved between black and white in South Africa, the solution will not be improved or made easier by a subjection of the blacks. The law of nature will take its course, and if the two races do not agree South Africa will either become essentially a European colony or remain a black man's land. Short of massacres, wars, and the tolerance of vice, there can be no check to the growth of native population. Therefore, if we have to live with him and eventually deal with him and take him into consultation, it is better to have an enlightened being to arrange matters with than a brutal savage swayed by a few professional agitators. It therefore follows that facilities of education to those natives seeking it should be granted, and those capable and willing to pay for tuition, by labour and otherwise, should even be taught trades. It does not follow that with an acknowledgment of the right and justice of educating the native that he should be sent to college by the Government and receive the education of a gentleman's son without first earning his living like the rest of us. A system of gratuitously educating the native before he has learned habits of industry would be a policy of Utopian generosity and productive of more evil than good. But the provision of educational facilities at centres of employment, as at the mines and in the towns of South Africa, especially in the nature of night or Sunday schools, under undenominational direction, is quite another and more reasonable and advantageous proposition than the system of rearing natives as exotics and estranging them from both their black brethren and white masters, which is the effect that past mission teaching has had upon native scholars.

It is not unreasonable to conclude that the result of such a leavening by education of the black mass of untutored labour employed at the mines and elsewhere would be a more staple and stable supply. Fewer desertions would ensue, higher appreciation of earnings, more wants and desires, and the adoption of a recognised calling. It would put the colour question to a crucial test, for should these advantages be unavailing, it might well be assumed that the case of the native to survive as the fittest is a poor one. On the other hand, should it succeed, it would have the effect of reconciling the African statesman to contemplating a bi-racial community, with the levelling so gradual as to deprive the movement of cataclysm or racial upheaval. Epitomised, the principle expounded is that education assists labour and industry and ignorance obstruct it.

An important factor towards the emancipation of the native from his present low social and intellectual stage is greater need, more ambitions. If the ideal to strive for (as is sometimes contended) is fewer wants and primitive conditions, then human progress is all humbug; we would revert to the Adam and Eve stage and discourage scientific discoveries, splendid architecture, and the pursuit of other worlds to conquer: the ox in the field would be envied. As want and ambitions are the incentives to human advancement, therefore with the native also wants and ambitions must be aroused. There seems no warrant, from any standpoint and from even a purely selfish point of view, why the South African native should be an exception to this operation. As the days of slavery are accounted as days of the past, unless the native problem is to be shelved or ignored and the present state deemed satisfactory, measures must be taken to properly guide and lead the native trend to mutual safety and satisfaction. As a means to a better end than obtains at present, the native should be encouraged to clothe himself decently —not necessarily on the European model—to cook decently, to aspire to better habitations than a straw hut, and otherwise require the simple luxuries or necessities of a civilised worker. As in all tropical and semi-tropical climes, in South Africa the conditions of aboriginal life are so easy, and the bodily requirements so few, that a couple of months' labour provides the annual equipment of the ordinary native. The object should therefore be to increase his wants, and, by introducing as early as possible the simple luxuries of civilised life, arouse in him some sort of emulation for the possession of worldly goods. Only contact with civilisation will do this, and the branch of civilisation the most needed is commerce, in the shape of the trader, farmer, and pioneer. The missionary is too apt to regard the Bible as the be-all and end-all of human happiness for savages. The wider problems of life and social responsibilities are, if not altogether ignored, yet neglected in favour of a denominational education and sundry surface observances. The real pioneer of civilisation, as the colonist understands it, is the trader or squatter, who arrives among the tribesmen and by precept and example, by trading or farming, excites the imitative attributes of the aboriginal native. Desire creates efforts to satisfy it, and soon leads the native to work.

The problem of the South African native is so greatly prominent in the one and immediate aspect that its extensive fringes receive little attention. The native we discuss and deal with is simply the unit of a horde or mass of 'raw' natives without established vocation or definite aims and ideals. The mass is still a drifting one, and not pressing in any given direction to a definite goal. If it were imbued with a common purpose or subject to common pressure, then it would be necessary to select a policy for present and future adoption in order to reduce the impact. At present the substance may be examined and dealt with in a state of flux or solution; it is not yet rigid, or of that unwieldy and unmalleable character to make it imperative in its course. But tailing away from the main body are numerous subsidiary organisms working their course between the crevices and divisions of the European classes and communities, their presence not felt until the reconstruction or development of the commune necessitates deeper probing into the structural basis of South African society. We refer to the classes of coloured people such as the Cape boy, the half-caste, the educated Kafir; the coloured landowner, tradesman and shopkeeper. These are the voortrekkers of the great black commando which is to invade a large portion of, if not overrun, the domain of the present European colonist, and when matters of franchise or municipal regulations come up for con-

sideration the presence of these growing links between
barbarism and civilisation is acutely realised.

That, with or without Government encouragement,
an increasing number of natives are emancipating
themselves from savagery is very patent. Men versed in
South African affairs are alive to the fact that behind
the immediately pressing problems of mining, settlement, and labour are others just now slumbering, but
merely waiting the opportunity to enter into the sphere
of problems requiring solution. The note has been
sounded in *Izwi Labantu* ('Hear the People!' or
'The Voice of the People'), a journal published at
East London, Cape Colony, and the organ of some
thousands of civilised Colony Kafirs of the Amaxosa
and kindred tribes. It is noteworthy to remark that
civilisation and religion have made their mark on the
natives to some, though in the aggregate really not
very considerable, extent in every region under occupation in South Africa. In the districts of East
London, Grahamstown, King William's Town, and
surrounding localities—a country thickly populated with
natives of a pure Kafir type—a considerable impression
has been made in the mass as in the individual. Kafirs in
European clothing are there as common as gooseberries
in England. Native churches abound in every town,
village, and rural centre, while natives with considerable wealth are neither rare nor strange. The feature
which distinguishes this portion of the Cape from other
localities where natives do congregate is not the mere
matter of adopting European garb and customs, but
the growing homogeneity of the mass, tending towards
consolidation of thought. The great Mission Station
of Lovedale, at Alice, near King William's Town, has

been a fruitful means towards this end, having achieved a position somewhat of the character of a native university and centre of native thought, with a corresponding effect upon the masses of natives residing around. The mission was founded and is under the control of the Presbyterian Free Church. Besides this greatly successful educationary enterprise, others of the Wesleyan community and the Church of England are doing similar work in the district. The immediate products of this one exceptional success in missionary enterprise—exceptional as stamping its teaching upon the mass coming under its influence, and not merely training a few stray individuals, as is the effect in other missionary centres—are the native pastor with clerical ambition and the native editor with great political aspirations. One organ of native opinion, under the editorship of Mr. Tengo Jabavu, had to be suppressed for inflammatory language during the *régime* of martial law. Although the natives as a class are overwhelmingly in favour of British rule as against Dutch or Bond rule, for some occult reason Mr. Tengo Jabavu took a contrary course in the *Imvo*, of which journal he was editor. The franchise in the Colony permits of a vote to the native, as to the European, showing a minimum qualification of 75*l.* annual income, which opens the ballot to a considerable number of natives in the regions specified. In a memorial forwarded last year to the Imperial authorities, representing the danger of retrogressive measures against the natives following a federated South Africa, *Izwi Labantu* has already given concrete expression to this slumbering force of educated native opinion. We qualify the opinion as 'educated' quite advisedly,

for even those with a mere superficial knowledge of
South African native affairs are perfectly aware that
by no stretch of imagination can the opinions as registered be judged as representative of common native
thought. The voices of the few who sound the note
are quite lost in the volume of chatter which springs
from the native kraal from the Cape to the Zambesi.
And the chatter is not about the franchise or the danger
of the franchise being suppressed or limited by colonial
federation. The significance of the petition is not,
however, lost. Though at the rate that conditions are
developing to-day many years must elapse before 'the
native peril' will enter into the domain of practical
politics in elections, yet what has been accomplished
in one region of South Africa may be, and one might
say is, expected to take place elsewhere. Though a
controlling native vote is figuratively and literally a
cloud of a dark hue still below the sky-line, its due
appearance on the horizon may be predicted for some
future date. The danger is not so deemed by the mere
fact that the elements are black. The position in the
United States provides some assurance that there will
be no pre-eminence of the negro and kindred races
over the European. But the danger lies in the psychological tendency of the black to blindly follow any
extreme if once moved by racial sympathy. It would
be as difficult under existing circumstances to inspire
with a common object, say, a Zulu, a Basuto, and a
Swazi, or a Xosa and a Bechuana, as it would to mix
oil and water. The tendency has always been to
heterogeneity in African native polity and not to homogeneity. But occasions arise in the case of great popu-
lations of African aborigines when a movement once

initiated, either through its inherent adaptability to native conditions and native thought or to the genius of the founder, obtains sufficient momentum at the outset to increase its ratio to the extent of cohering a large section of the outlying native tribes. Only a short time ago one was startled at learning of an Ethiopian movement engineered by an American black pastor in South Africa favouring such a consolidation, and at any time, conditions being in its favour, some similar quasi-religious or quasi-political movement, or partaking of both, may be started by a more than usually ambitious and talented native teacher developed in the higher missionary schools.

We do not deduce from these forebodings that the policy of educating the native is a bad one. Education, properly rendered, can never harm any one, and tends to the advantage of the community. But the conclusion the deduction leads to is that together with the knowledge of religion and of politics must be inculcated loyalty to the flag and loyalty to the Colonial Government ; the virtue and necessity of work and of obedience.

The United States have a kindred problem to solve —kindred in the sense that it is also a question of sentiment, racial antipathy, or perhaps, more happily expressed, racial divisions, and a question of colour. But in the United States the negro population is a rooted exotic ; in South Africa the position is reversed, and the Europeans are the exotic, and the blacks the primal basic element occupying the soil. That neither are precisely the original element does not affect the question. Some years ago it was considered that the United States had solved once and for all the racial

question, and that equal liberty and opportunity were
to be given to black and to white. This, however, does
not appear to be the case after all. Here, at this late
date, some years after the emancipation of the blacks,
controversy is again aroused, and not a little bad blood
evoked between the opposed ideals. As President
Roosevelt is accounted one of the most distinguished
thinkers of the day, and a man of great parts and
robust opinions, it is interesting to learn his views on a
question fraught with so much peril to South Africa.
In a letter written to Mr. Clark Howell, editor of the
Atlanta Constitution, a leading Southern paper, he
says, in making negro appointments, ' the prime tests
' I have applied have been those of character, fitness,
' and ability, and when I have been dissatisfied with
' what has been offered me in my own party lines I have
' without hesitation gone to the opposite party. I cer-
' tainly cannot treat mere colour as a bar to holding
' office any more than I could so treat creed or birth-
' place, always providing that in other respects the
' applicant or incumbent is a worthy and well-behaved
' American citizen.' It is noteworthy that this stand
for political and social equality of the black when
otherwise fitted—for that is what it means despite
President Roosevelt's politic disclaimer—should have
to be made in the States at this late stage. Evidently
the people of the Transvaal are not of this opinion.
Despite the recommendation and efforts of Lord
Milner he could not persuade the popular representatives in the Council to subscribe to the principle of
granting a municipal franchise to educated blacks, or
coloured men of any race. In this matter the Press
and the public of Johannesburg stand rigid. Residing

amid a great native population still steeped in the darkness of savagery, they fear that a loophole for the entry of the advanced guard will end in complete capitulation to the mob. We think the fear is ill-founded, at least as far as the African native is concerned. Before such tests as educational and property qualifications will be passed by the African native in any material numbers much water will have flowed through London Bridge. Before the time arrives that a material proportion of the natives achieve such standards the battle between sane conservatism and blind unreasoning fear and prejudice will have been fought and lost. The best method to avert the flood is by sluice-gates and lock. It is wiser to permit the few of the highest strata to percolate through and keep the stream at a normal level than to block the road and provoke a violent bursting of the barriers.

That even in Johannesburg, amid the great number of raw and uncivilised natives, a community exists of superior plane of thought and yet in touch with the lower masses is evidenced in a demonstration which took place on the outskirts of the Johannesburg Location this year to commemorate the entry of Lord Roberts' forces into Johannesburg and the release of the natives commandeered by the Boer forces. The ceremony took the shape of a thanksgiving service. As described in a local journal : ' Each minute brought its fresh quota of worshippers, and soon nearly a thousand men and women, not to mention the piccaninnies, must have been assembled. The main body of the congregation formed a large circle, inside which was the minister and others who were to conduct the proceedings. Only one of the organs was used, and

seated alongside it was a small choir, whilst not far
removed was a band under Mr. Jas. D. Ngojo. The
instruments were few, but effective, and conspicuous
among them were the cornets. Altogether the scene
was distinctly impressive, and to the knot of white
people gathered on the fringe of the crowd most interesting. The service was conducted by the Rev. W.
B. Rubusani, Congregational minister of East London,
earnestness and fervour characterising the attitude
of the congregation. Quite a pleasing feature was the
music. The King Edward Darkies B.B. and choir,
although not numerous, led with good effect, the voices
of the choir harmonising well. Several chants were
given, evidently of a joyous description, and here the
voices were heard to the greatest advantage. Very
little of the proceedings could be understood by the
white people, although two words stood out un-
mistakably—"Lord Milner." It was plain that the
natives were remembering the Governor in their
petitions, as well as the great *inkose*, King Edward.
The first sermon was preached by the Rev. W. B.
Rubusani with an eloquence that impressed his hearers.
His theme was suggested by the welcome change that
had taken place in native policy since the new *régime*.
He was followed by Mr. Sortonga, a man with grey
hair and a short grey beard, who was clearly regarded
with much respect. He emphasised the points of the
Rev. W. B. Rubusani, and was in his turn succeeded
by a colleague, who supplied the one dramatic incident
of the gathering. Calling to mind the ill-treatment
suffered under the Boers by many of his compatriots,
he described particularly how one had been sjam-
bokked. His address moved his audience, and wailing

and weeping were heard by the waters of the vlei.
The end came shortly afterwards in the shape of a
good collection. Saucers were handed around, but
many walked to a table in the centre and deposited
their sixpences and shillings. A second meeting was
held in the afternoon.'

It is not very probable that all these natives were
Makolwes, or Christian Kafirs, but the account well
tallies with our assumption that at the psychological
moment leaders of education may be forthcoming to
sway the native mind in a given direction, and it is for
the Europeans to see to it that the bent of the superior
class of natives is not directed by a sense of injustice
into dangerous channels. At the last annual conference of the South African Teachers' Association,
held at Capetown, the Rev. Mr. Taylor, of Lovedale
Institution, read a paper by the Rev. D. D. Stormont
on ' Native Education.' In this paper it is shown that
the ' educated boys ' are already becoming a factor in
native treatment. Already over 90,000 children are
attending school. It is asserted that these figures
sweep away all objections of a doctrinaire type, and
blow to shreds all unpractical theories of the past or
of the present. ' Native education is a solid fact and a
political force growing in power in the country. You
cannot put back the clock without a social or a political revolution. In fifty years or so Kafir will be
hard pressed for existence, as hard as Gaelic or Welsh,
Manx or Erse is at the present day. Then Kafir
societies will take the place of Celtic and Kailyaird
coteries, and the Kafir renaissance and influence will
be duly chronicled in English literature. But it is
acknowledged that the present curriculum is rather a

stiff one for native schools. Teachers find it the
hardest work imaginable to get up their pupils for
examinations upon the syllabuses of the Education
Department and the University. The standard of pass
in higher work is so high that very few natives have
been able to reach a bare pass.' Which bears out our
contention that the intellectual supremacy of the
European is not at stake.

Mr. Booker T. Washington, whose genius for negro
education is acknowledged in the States, and whose
services have been sought in treating the native problem in South Africa by Earl Grey, said in one of his
frank and impressive addresses on behalf of his Tuskegee
Institute : 'I want to show you negroes who stand at
' the front in the affairs of state, religion, education,
' mechanics, commerce, and household economy. By
' this sign we shall conquer. By this method we
' shall so knit our civil and business interests into
' that of the white man that when he prospers we
' shall prosper ; when we fail, he fails. . . . We are
' coming 8,000,000 strong by the way of the college,
' by the way of agriculture, the shop, the factory,
' the trades, the household arts. . . . This is the true
' emancipation.' This is the gospel of work and education which has made this unique negro teacher famous.
That a dawning ambition for another and better life
is in the thought of the native is shown in the following
exhortation of the Rev. Jeremiah Mzimba, a native
preacher, speaking at Mafeking Location : 'Look how
' solidly united all the white races are in this country.
' Let us follow their example and I have no doubt that
' by exerting our abilities we will apply a fresh stimulus
' to the beginning already made. This will enable us

' to raise various tradesmen, handicrafts, and scientific
' agriculturists, who will supply other parts of the
' country with the products of the land, and find the
' money to elevate the race into higher stages of
' civilisation and education. Let us all unite upon this
' point, and a solid combination of the black races of
' this country will assure our progress.' This is the
writing on the wall, and points to a future period when
the character of the native will change. But at the
present the sort of native depicted in these lines is a
hidden factor, and does not bulk in the average
colonial's attention. For the ultimate lot, mission, or
development of the South African native is darkly
shrouded in the future. He starts without the incubus
of Mohammedanism or any trammels of ingrained
Paganism. His mind is a blank ready to absorb the
most modern conception of Christianity, though perhaps
by inherited temperament the supernatural more than
the philosophical attributes will prevail. He shows
little or no signs of declining in physique or prolifical-
ness. The Bantu type is distinct from the negro of
more northern climes, and might quite conceivably
prove a higher type. The failure of the negro in the
States may quite possibly prove no precedent upon
which to base the future of the Bantu in South Africa.
Though his ultimate stage is not to be even approximated, yet one thing is fairly clear—that his complete
metamorphosis, should it come about, is a matter of
generations, perhaps of centuries.

For in the tortuous road towards advancement it is
vain to expect one continuous upward trend. Just as
the line of advancement will take varied turns, so will
the level not always be on the up-grade, though higher

altitudes be reached.   As familiarity with European
customs and mode of thought progresses, the *evil* which
underlies much of our boasted civilisation will affect
the native with the *good*.   This tendency to assimilate
indiscriminately European attributes, words, and action
recalls the account of an early British explorer among
the islands of the Pacific.   He touched an island and
was soon surrounded by a horde of unsophisticated
natives headèd by their chief.   For some time greetings
were more expressive in grins than in words, for
neither race understood the other.   But fortunately
the chief bethought him of a native who had returned
to his island after some months of service among the
white men.   The native was duly summoned and the
chief commanded him to converse with the Europeans
and discover their errand and pleasure.   The 'travelled'
islander in perfect good faith and confidence fired a
volley of all the words he could recall from the voca-
bulary of the crew under whom he served.   *They
consisted of a string of oaths*, hurled vehemently at the
astonished person of the officer.   But the situation was
grasped, and the air waxed blue with the lurid language
of the two spokesmen.   The story is very characteristic.   In South Africa, unhappily, some of the earliest
words picked up by the native are not complimentary,
consisting in most cases of those by which his white
ganger curses his clumsiness.   Colonial experience has
taught that with the acquisition of Christianity and
civilisation enter such evils as impudence, modern craft
grafted upon native duplicity, ill-discipline, and carnal
desire in forbidden directions.   During the last session
of the Rhodesian Legislative Council some very im-
passioned speeches were delivered upon the social evil

rearing its head in that country in the form of assaults by natives upon European women, with criminal intent. Some very horrible cases had come to light, having the effect of stirring the anger of the colonists to boiling-point, culminating in one instance in an attempt to lynch the culprit by suddenly lassoing him in Court and dragging him to an improvised gallows. As a result of the growing evil, pressure was brought on the Government by the elected members in the Legislative Council to pass a law imposing death as the penalty on those found guilty.

Arising from the subject under discussion some very serious charges were hurled against the methods of the missionary. It was urged by Mr. Frames, and strongly contended by Mr. Holland, both members of the Legislative Council for Matabeleland, that this and other growing evils of the civilised native are in great part due to the teaching of the missionary, who, they contend, merely endows the savage with the veneer of civilisation—whilst disturbing his native qualities—instead of radically altering his thought and trend. And common reason supports this view, which is so widely held by the colonist. You may take a raw savage and clothe him and teach him to read and write and to pray. All this may be done in the course of a few months or a few years. But it is not to be expected that you can develop a trained and inherited savage into a child of civilisation in thought and action in a decade, or, in the mass, in a century—except, perhaps, in those rare cases where a black infant is bred and brought up solely in contact with Europeans. There may be exceptions, but they are so rare that they firmly establish the rule. That Christianity and

civilisation must tend to moral betterment, where only
vice or a mental blank is presented to the operator, is
a truism ; but in the case of the raw South African
native the material upon which the missionary operates
is neither vice undiluted nor does it lack intelligence.
The average South African savage has a fair portion of
intelligence, and in many cases great intelligence, while
his morals are in some aspects higher than those of
the average civilised man. Dignity, simplicity, discipline, honour, chastity, and obedience are striking
traits of the raw Kafir.

In the case of the ' social pest '—the one evil
which angers the European to boiling-point—it is the
spurious imitation of this Christian type which stands
prominent—the savage clothed in veneer and not the
transformed personality. In every mission station for
the one convert turned out with developed thought and
earnest and Christian desire hundreds leave the fold
with a bare covering of civilised garb—having lost the
pristine excellence of tribal ethics and gained the restless desire and ambition of the struggling European,
with a vague notion of equality with his white brethren
and a settled determination to assert it whenever he
can with personal safety. From this class springs a
large proportion of the ' social pests,' who regard a
white woman as their peer, and look her boldly in the
face. Rare, indeed, is it that the better-disciplined
raw savage contemplates such an act as an assault
upon a white woman. In fact, the tribes of the Zulu
stock in their pristine state regard with horror any
contact with a white skin. It is easily seen by these circumstances that the coloured question in South Africa
differs in degree and condition from those the European

has been accustomed to in past colonisation. The
many phases of psychical evolution which present themselves in the future of the blacks of South Africa have
the greatest interest to the sociologist and the politician.

The presence of this mere 'veneer' in Christian or
civilised natives is one discerned and commented on by
all thoughtful South African writers on native life and
thought. Mrs. Martin, in her excellent little book on
Basutoland, drawing upon her experiences gathered
while residing in that territory, says : ' The missionaries
' undoubtedly do an enormous amount of good, but many
' of them are as unwise in their treatment of the Basutos
' as the Boers, though they err on the side of kind-
' ness. They fail to realise that civilisation *must* come
' gradually to be effective ; that to try to run and jump
' before you can walk is foolish, and may often be harm-
' ful, and by treating a raw native as an equal they are
' very possibly laying the foundation-stone for native
' disturbances in the future. Directly a native begins
' to look upon himself as an educated being, equal to
' the white man, in ninety-nine cases out of a hundred
' he at once loses all respect for the European, whom he
' treats in an offhand, condescending manner, intensely
' offensive to any one who has realised the wide gulf
' which separates the two races. So many people fail
' to understand that a South African native, even the
' best, cannot be placed in the same category as an
' Indian. I firmly believe that kindness will repay us
' infinitely better than cruelty ; *but* it must be kindness
' mixed with *great* firmness, and there should be *no*
' lowering of the master to the level of the native.'
These conclusions embody the thought of all colonists
having large experience among natives.

A Commission has already been appointed to consider the native question broadly from a South African point of view, from which much is expected. The Commission, to be successful, will have to bring itself, in the first place, to the frame of mind to recognise that the native population of South Africa intend to stay. There appear no signs of the native retiring before civilisation either through physical deterioration or failing powers of increase. We do not say from an egoistic point of view that deterioration and diminution would not be the best solution from the standpoint of the European. But even those who view the Kafir as a superfluity would scarcely countenance any artificial measures tending to his suppression. If he has to stay and be with us, the best policy is to boldly face the fact and influence him to spheres of better usefulness than he fills at present. The entrance of the native in the political sphere is merely a matter of time. Already at the Cape the thin end of the wedge is inserted, and the 'coloured' vote is an object of strife between the political parties. That, failing some natural influence affecting the increase of the African native, the coloured people will eventually become a political power is very plain to the student, always providing their mental powers are adequate to achieve the necessary educationary qualification. That many already possess these qualifications tends to show that the necessary plane will be reached. It is therefore essential that in considering any concerted scheme of government of the natives this condition of the future should be borne in mind. If the Commission should find it more convenient to ignore the distant danger and merely recommend legislation for the day, then the result will be legislation lagging behind development, and more acute conditions arising than would have been possible under an intelligent policy. An opportunity now offers of grasping the native question firmly, and propounding a system of treatment leading to racial amity, while drawing a long line of division and probation only to be surmounted by the best of the inferior class, yet not insurmountable to the extent of forbidding all hope under normal and peaceful progress.

PART II

MINES AND LABOUR

CHAPTER VIII

NATIVE LABOUR THE ROOT FACTOR

ALL South African economic questions tend to the conclusion that the crux of South African progress—
political, social, and economic—rests in the Native
Labour Question. Just as the Rand mining industry
is the heart and the nerve centre of South African
trade, so is native or raw labour the final arbiter of
the healthy potentialities of the great feeder. This
axiom has been acknowledged in the weighty articles
dealing with South African trade development contributed by Mr. Benjamin Kidd to the *Times*. It is
also confirmed by every authority making inquiry on
the spot.

Why in South Africa such a unique condition
should prevail, compared with other large mining and
industrial centres scattered over the earth's surface,
wherein black or coloured labour is essential to
European progress, is too deep and prolific a subject
to merely skim with any degree of satisfaction within
these limits. Perhaps the general principle moving

human progress, that the greater the obstacle to a desirable consummation the greater the effort to obtain it, and, conversely, the greater the natural facilities of satisfying human ends, the less the effort, and therefore the less the brain quality developed, may be applied in explanation ; though difficulties enow have been encountered in the pursuit of wealth and settlement in South Africa. The coloured races of Australia and North America, unlike the natives of Africa, were ill prepared or equipped by temperament to peacefully and resignedly adapt themselves to European civilisation and commercial activity. Also the climates in these regions lent themselves more readily to European life and conditions. In South America a half-caste race was evolved at the expense of the European strain, which has more or less satisfactorily solved the difficulty; but in South Africa not only has the native sturdily resisted the corrosive and disintegrating influences of civilisation, but the natural conditions and climate of his land have proved effectual allies in his efforts. The result of this new departure in European colonisation has created the real factor which has tended to so sharply demark the spheres of native and European activity. As neither the climate nor the absence of raw labour has compelled the European to shoulder the burden of pick and shovel or plough, he has slipped quietly and complacently into the position of overseer and designer. Means were found ready at hand to obtain his ends by the free use of the fund of cheap and simple labour lying around him, which he has for so long utilised and accustomed himself to that without it he is lost. This has been the paramount influence in retarding Boer cultivation of the soil, and, paradoxically, at the same time the paramount means of tilling it. Without slaves and native labour in the early days it is conceivable that the Cape Colony and the late Orange Free State would ere this have developed into another agricultural Australia and California ; with the labour available all efforts have been stunted in growth by the great facilities of the environment, and a life of ease became part of the recognised features of farmer or Boer life. In the gold and the diamond fields, similarly, the presence of native labour provided no necessity for European unskilled labour, and the system which has developed is altogether based upon an adequate native supply.

Whether this real weakness in South African economics is an exotic growth, or inherently due to the economical, ethnological, physical, and geographical features of the land ; whether it is an insidious parasite or a fundamental obstacle ; the time has approached when the conditions have again changed, and the earlier facilities of obtaining labour have given way to a period of urgently requiring labour. It is estimated in a recent collation of the native population, based upon the most recent returns available—which in all cases in South Africa must of necessity be taken as approximate—that the number of natives south of the Zambesi, including Portuguese territory, totals between seven and eight millions. It is now estimated that within a few years some 320,000 boys will be required on the Rand to keep the 16,000 stamps going as predicted for the future. Taking the proportion of one in eight of the native population as subject to the desire to work away from their homes, it is seen that about one-third of the total native labouring population

would be required for the Rand. But the demands of
the Rand, large as they are, are small in comparison
with the demands from other centres and spheres of
activity, taken in the aggregate. There are the goldfields of Rhodesia and of Barberton; of Kimberley
and of the coal mines; of the railways and of the
ports; of agriculture and the towns—in fact, on the
system at present in vogue in South Africa every
additional white man will require from three to five
blacks directly or indirectly ministering to his needs.
To satisfy this present and growing demand, and, at
the same time, provide for the increasing tendency of
blacks to leave the ranks of raw labour and adopt some
branch of skilled labour, one of three conditions must
develop. Either the natural increase of the black
must satisfy the increasing shortage, or other coloured
natives will have to be imported, or the European will
have to scratch for himself. In considering the near
future, with which we may legitimately deal, it is not
to be expected that such a radical change would at
once come over the land as the adoption of European
labour, displacing in one fell swoop the blacks. The
slow and gradual adoption by the European of the
principle of living by the sweat of his brow may ensue,
but against its universal application is the growth of
the black population (which, though perhaps insufficient to supply the whole needs in raw labour, would
always press against an European invasion of its
accustomed realm), climatic drawbacks, and prejudices
of the colonists in respect to colour. Limits may be
legitimately assigned to the expansion of European
labour in the face of a settled and growing native
community. With regard to the increase of native

population, should it continue in normal ratio with that of the whites, the start with which greatly growing mining and agricultural developments endow Demand is likely to keep it ahead of naturally growing Supply. The next generation of blacks in their increase will probably be co-existent with a three- or five-fold increase in mining, commerce, and agriculture, and together with this overlapping of demand on native labour resources will travel the growing tendency of the black to desert in part the old path of universal navvydom. The condition in South Africa is as if in England, with its present population, the upper ten or twenty thousand were numbered by the million, and were accustomed to the arbitrarily disposed and restricted raw labour of the working classes. Such a condition can never persist, even in a mixed community of blacks and whites. It is seen, consequently, that in the near future either the European must in part carry out the duties hitherto confined to the native, or that another source of raw labour supply will have to be located and drawn upon from outside. It almost appears that the last-mentioned conditions will soon have to be faced. It is just as vain to expect the European to suddenly change his custom of employing blacks to do the rough and unskilled labour as it is to expect the black to forthwith take cheerily to labour and finally desert his life of simple idleness at the kraals. Both changes entail a process of gradual evolution, and in the interim a way out of the difficulty must be found. By some it is contended that the fears of a permanent and increasingly deficient supply of native labour are premature and unfounded. It is urged that certain extraordinary factors now reigning

are the real cause of the shyness of labour, such as
money freely earned during the war, reaping of crops,
and the disturbance still prevailing as an aftermath of
the late conflict. Yet, if we take the figures quoted as
reliable, it is difficult to see'how all demands are going
to be satisfied anyhow. It may happen that the gold
industry on the Rand and in Rhodesia will not progress
at the expected rate, and the land generally to the extent
predicted. Assuming a more moderate rate of industrial
expansion, the labour question may not prove acute ;
but the popular impression, with the imprimatur of Sir
David Barbour's experience and foresight, is the
reverse. As the Transvaal is the pivot of South African
progress, and just as the Boer rule is to the British,
and past trade to future trade in South Africa, so one
may reasonably assume that the net commercial result
will be commensurate with the administrative difference. The gold is just as rich and just as available as
it was then, and still in accessible quantities for years
to come. As under the Boer the native supply was
inadequate, so will it appear to be under the British,
with all the recent developments added.

The importance and true bearings of the African
native labour question upon South African industrial
progress have been seized by Mr. Chamberlain with his
usual directness and acumen. Speaking in the House
of Commons when the subject came up for discussion
this session (1903), Mr. Chamberlain said : ' The whole
' of South Africa at the present time is more or less de-
' pendent for its future prosperity on the Transvaal. In
' the Transvaal there has been in the course of a few
' years a gigantic development of a great industry, as the
' result of which tens of thousands of British workmen

' of the very best class have left their own country and
' permanently established themselves there. Great
' towns have sprung up out of the veld with large
' industries which are contingent upon the main in-
' dustry. Everywhere is to be seen development, and it
' is all due to this one industry ; and the men who by
' their skill, capital, industry, and knowledge—not for
' philanthropic motives, but with the idea of filling their
' own pockets—have brought this about ought not to be
' treated as pariahs, and as if they were doing what was
' not for the advantage of the country. That is an
' absurd position to take up, and in future do let us
' leave the mine-owners alone, and let us treat them
' with the same kindly respect with which we treat
' coal-owners, cotton-spinners, bankers or financiers, or
' anybody else engaged in using his brains to make his
' fortune.' Repeating that the prosperity of the country
depended upon the progress of the great mining
industry, and that it was not to the interest of the
British Government or people to do anything to discourage it, but to do everything possible to develop it,
the right hon. gentleman continued : 'You want to
' develop the other industries of the country, which are
' very important, but I believe you will not do so for a
' long time. Not for years or cycles will you develop its
' agricultural resources. Every one knows that there are
' vast areas of country which only want expenditure
' upon irrigation to make them as fertile as Egypt itself.
' That means, in the first place, a demand for the
' produce of the land ; and, in the second place, capital
' in large quantities for the purpose of developing it. I
' say, then, let us treat this question of native labour

' without any prejudice, and simply in connection with
' the general prosperity of the country.'

Mr. Lionel Phillips, writing to the *Times* on the
Labour Question, says : ' On the question of obtaining
' an adequate supply of labour for the gold mines and
' other industries depends not only the welfare of the
' mine-owners, but the advancement of South African
' development, the increase of British trade which will
' follow in its wake, and the provision of the greater
' revenues which will be needed in the Transvaal to
' meet all its obligations.'

Against these reasoned conclusions showing the
paramount importance of the gold industry to South
Africa, the most tangible argument advanced by those
who seek to minimise their importance and the consequent
necessity to adopt heroic measures to provide the necessary labour is the absurd contention that as the gold
does not spoil in the keeping, and the smaller the output the longer the life of the Rand, therefore by the
lack of labour the Transvaal really does not suffer in the
end.

This thesis has been seriously advanced in Parliament
by a statesman of post-Ministerial rank such as Sir John
Gorst, and has been stated independently in South Africa
by the *South African News* of Bond proclivity. The
contention is not worthy of serious criticism, else were
it a debatable point whether it is wise to make the most
of any industry. It is also urged that mining arrogantly
usurps the position of agriculture as a fundamental
factor towards industrial progress. That after the
mines are worked out agriculture will always remain
the basis of political wealth. Waiving the circumstance that with the present state of labour supply

the depletion of the ever-descending lodes is a matter of generations, the fact always remains that in our time, and probably long after we are gone, the basis of South African wealth will lie with the minerals—as far as human thought can pierce to-day.

But not only the mines depend mainly upon native labour for development, agriculture throughout the land suffers in similar form though not to the same extent, due to the pastoral native being but a poor agriculturist. Quite recently a Sneeuwburg farmer, writing to *Onze Courant*, made the following doleful lament.

' Here we are on our farms,' says he, ' with more
' work than we can attend to, but no servants.   Taxes
' must be paid to the Government, and the country must
' be assisted to go ahead.   As farmers, we must produce
' wool and grain—in fact, all that the country possibly
' can produce—in order to make it fruitful, not only for
' the farmers, but also for townsfolk ; and what support
' do we get from the Government ?   Go to the town
' locations, yes, go right into the towns themselves, and
' you will find Kafirs and Hottentots in dozens and half-
' dozens without work and without money.   Now I ask
' what do they live on ?   And can our Government do
' nothing to make these loafers work, nothing to compel
' those who stand idle in the village to leave the place ?
' Of late the Kafirs and Hottentots have become con-
' firmed in their laziness, and not only is this to the dis-
' advantage of land and people, but it is a grievous
' offence in the sight of God.   I trust that the municipal
' authorities will move in the matter, and that our Go-
' vernment will render them all assistance.   I also hope
' that our members of Parliament will exert themselves
' in this connection, for surely it is nothing more than

' right that we, as farmers, should be supported, for are
' we not the backbone of the land?'

This may not be taken as an isolated case. The
lament is only one of many which continually crop up
in the Cape Colony. At the recent Bond Congress
similar complaints were uttered of want of farm labour
and the apathy of the Government, while Colonel
Stanford, Chief Inspector in the Transkeian territories
of the Cape Colony, in an official report contained in a
Blue-book on native affairs for 1903, stated that : 'The
' question of a labour supply for this colony (I am not
' now referring to a supply for the Rand) is a most
' serious one, and is of very much more importance than
' many of the questions exercising the minds of our
' legislators, for unless the farmers of our colony can
' obtain sufficient native labour to carry out the neces-
' sary work on the land, a very large number of the farms
' will be thrown out of cultivation altogether, whilst
' many others will only be partially cultivated, thus re-
' ducing the food supply. The cultivation of the land
' is of paramount importance to the public, especially in
' view of the large influx of population which is going
' on, and the high cost of the necessaries of life. I am
' not prepared to indicate the lines upon which this state
' of matters is to be remedied. I leave it to the united
' wisdom of our members of Parliament to formulate a
' scheme for solving this vital question. I bring the
' matter forward as one that must, in the interests of the
' country, sooner or later receive the earnest attention
' of the Legislature.'

Accentuating this official warning, last June, labour
for the agricultural and horticultural industries of
the Cape Colony was discussed at a meeting of the

Western Province Horticultural Board. The prospects of obtaining Italian labourers, and the feasibility of importing Kabyles (from Northern Africa), Swiss, or Frisians, were considered. Finally, it was resolved to call the attention of Parliament to the fact that the efforts to import Italian labour had not been successful up to the present, and to express the hope that a vote would be passed by the House for the purpose of importing suitable agricultural labour from any part of the world. It was pointed out that by the expression ' any part of the world ' the Chinese would be included, but it was decided not to alter the decision, inasmuch as the matter will be in the hands of the Secretary for Agriculture, who would be guided by public opinion.

If this is shown to be the case in the older colony, where natives for years have been dwelling among white men and are quite familiar with the work open for them, how much more cause have the agriculturists of the inland colonies to complain, with the large draughts on the available labour made by the mines. It is needless to add that the scarcity of agricultural labour is also a theme in these colonies.

In a speech delivered by Sir George Farrar at Driefontein, on the Rand, the popular mining leader produced some figures on Rand requirements which are worthy of record denoting the shortage : ' Number ' of stamp mills, and present and future requirements ' of native labour, for the gold mines of the Wit- ' watersrand, and coal mines, Transvaal, and for the ' town and suburbs of Johannesburg :—Stamp mills ' working, Witwatersrand, February 1903, 2,975 ; do., ' outside districts, 145 ; total, 3,120. Number of stamp ' mills working, Witwatersrand, 1899, 5,970 ; do., out-

' side districts, 400 ; total, 6,370. Number of stamp
' mills now erected, 6,500 ; do. in contemplation next
' 5 years, 5,300 ; total, 11,860.

' *Native Labour.*—Supply to-day : Natives em-
' ployed on gold mines, Witwatersrand, 53,375 ; do.
' coal mines, 6,796 ; total, 60,711. Supply required
' immediately : Total requirements, gold mines, Wit-
' watersrand, to-day, 141,250 ; do. coal mines, 10,000 ;
' total, 151,250. Deficiency in supply to-day : Present
' shortage of labour, gold mines, Witwatersrand, 87,880 ;
' do. coal mines, 3,204 ; total, 91,084. Native labour
' supply required 5 years hence : gold mines, Rand,
' 250,000 ; do. coal mines, 25,000 ; total, 275,000.

' Labour supply, town and suburbs, Johannesburg :
' 35,000 ; estimated number of natives required 5 years
' hence, 60,000.

' *Summary* : Deficiency of labour required to-day for
' coal and gold mines, 91,084 ; labour required 5 years
' hence for coal and gold mines, and Johannesburg and
' suburbs, 300,000. Add to these the requirements of
' labour for the construction of the lines as sanctioned
' by the Conference, which have been estimated at from
' 30,000 to 40,000 natives. To this again must be added
' the requirements, both agricultural and industrial, for
' the whole of South Africa.'

In comment Sir George stated : 'When one considers
' this absorption, and also what labour is now at work
' on the mines and in Johannesburg—and the various
' other towns in the Transvaal—one is led strongly to
' the opinion that there is almost the same amount of
' labour now working as before the war (despite the
' actual shortage).'

With regard to Rhodesia, the requirements have

been estimated by the president of the Chamber of
Mines, and are as follows :—' Southern Rhodesia : Able-
' bodied adult population, 110,000 (total population,
' 513,000). Present requirements : Mines, 16,335; other
' employment, 19,500; total, 35,835. Short of present
' requirements: Mines, 4,930; other employment, 2,500;
' total, 7,430. Actually at work, 28,405. Of which
' 14,550 are local natives and 13,846 are outside natives,
' total 28,405.

' Out of 11,405 boys at work to-day on the
' Rhodesian mines, only 1,779 are local boys. Future
' requirements : Mines, 25,000 ; other employment,
' 30,000 ; total, 55,000; plus present requirements
' 35,835, grand total 90,835.'

[In reproducing these and other figures dealing
with mines and labour it should be stated that the
book was written before the reports of the proceedings
of the Johannesburg Labour Commission became
available. Nothing, however, of material consequence
has transpired, throughout the exhaustive and volu-
minous evidence given, to render any need of revising
what was already in type on the subject.]

CHAPTER IX

THE DEMAND OF THE MINES

In considering the native question of South Africa the natural corollary to the subject is employment in the mines. This one sphere of employment overshadows in public interest all other vocations, and rightly so. Just as economic South Africa depends upon the prosperity of its gold industry (a postulate which few will be so bold as to deny), so does native employment in other spheres depend upon the native's willingness to serve in the mines. While it is important that native labour should be adequate in agriculture, in railway construction, and at the ports, it is positively essential that the mines should be satisfied. It is scarcely an exaggeration to declare that every throb of the Stock Exchange at Johannesburg has its responses in the four corners of the British South African realm. A lively market at Johannesburg circulates the life-blood of industry into every port and every centre; a stagnant market paralyses enterprise from Capetown to Durban. When Johannesburg enjoys a boom goods are in demand, buildings are constructed, theatres are full, produce is high-priced, hotels are crammed, and steamers are laden; Capetown and Durban are full of up-country visitors, on pleasure or business bent, Port Elizabeth has her quays crowded, the farmers are reaping rich

harvests, and public revenue expands. When Johannesburg is dull, goods are a glut, debts are bad, rents
shrink, competition becomes keen, hotel-takings fall
off, produce suffers from extreme fluctuation, indents
are cancelled, and the passenger-lists of the steamers
are blank. Though the effect may not be immediate,
for market fluctuations are expected and discounted—
times always varying somewhat—yet when the cause
is fundamental and the depression persistent the effect
on the outlying colonies is certain. In other gold-
mining countries the influences for evil to be taken
into account in current and prospective speculation are
such as the failure of a lode, labour strikes, financial
crises, and imperfect estimates of mining propositions.
On the Rand, due to the nature of the ore deposits and
the high standard of finance and management, such
influences have not a similar importance. The gold
industry of the Rand is now reduced to an exact
science. The banket deposits are proved to enormous
depths, labour strikes are unknown, capital is abundant,
finance is like a rock, and the quality of the lode is
stable. The closing down of a battery creates a
temporary discomfort, whether due to the ore being
worked out within the limit of the property (discounted
in advance and mathematically calculated) or to lack
of prudent stoping. Sometimes undue inflation of
values causes a set-back and a slump on the Exchange.
Political unrest temporarily restricts development, and
reckless speculation ends in disaster to the gambler.
But through all, the 6,500 stamps are rhythmically
beating, crushing the unfailing gold from the uniform
ore, and producing the customary returns. The one
vulnerable spot in the Rand armour is its need of raw

labour. The native alone has the power to cripple
this powerful industry that supplies life to South
Africa.

Many are the schemes that have been laid to
remedy this weakness. Some have suggested a freer
use of machinery. Others have prescribed more white
labour, while the consensus of mining opinion has
plumped for the Asiatic. A permanent native labour
supply has been sought in Portuguese East Africa, in
Uganda, in Nyassaland, and in British Central Africa.
Up to the present none of these sources have proved
feasible or sufficient for the purpose. Dealing with
the recommendation for the employment of more
and better machinery in order to lessen the necessity
for manual work, and the charge sometimes brought
against the mining industry that insufficient attention has been paid to this labour-saving medium, the
following extract from the descriptive and statistical
report on the Rand gold-mining industry, drawn up by
leading engineers and presented to Mr. Chamberlain,
makes reply :

' It has been the aim of the engineers here to make
' use of machinery and labour-saving devices to a greater
' extent than has ever before been employed in gold
' mining. That this is so is on the whole frankly
' admitted by engineers from other parts of the world.
' It is not claimed that all possible means of elucidating
' the labour problem by the application of mechanical
' devices have been exhausted. On the contrary, the
' necessity for still greater effort is fully recognised, and
' it is frankly acknowledged that in the matter of
' haulage, both under and over ground, there is scope
' for still greater improvement, but it may be confidently

' affirmed that nowhere in the world in metalliferous
' mines, with a thickness of deposit similar to the Rand,
' are labour-saving devices employed to a greater or
' even to the same extent, nor is there record of a thin-
' reef deposit being worked in a more energetic manner
' or on a greater scale, and on this account it has been
' possible to employ a great amount of white labour on
' a class of mechanical work which requires a higher
' grade of intelligence than is developed in the native.'

On the contention for the wider employment of
white labour the same authority emphasises the
great difficulty of whites and blacks working together.
Up to then 12,000 white men were being employed,
earning on an average 353l. a year. Where white
labour was employed in 1902, the cost of production
was 2s. 10d. per ton higher. In brief, the experiment of
white labour has proved unsatisfactory, as the skilled
white labourer has been unsettled, fearing a reduction
in pay, while the unskilled man has been dissatisfied,
as the wages he received were less than those of the
skilled. As a muscular machine, the best-developed
native is equal to the white man. It is hopeless
seriously to consider from an economical standpoint
the substituting of a mere muscular machine, costing
20s. or even 10s. a day, for one costing 2s. or 3s. If
white labour were adopted, the average cost per ton
would be increased by 10s. 1d. (The average dividend
per ton crushed has been 10s. 7d.) Half of the mines
would be worked without profit, and the remainder
would have to reduce their dividend by 44 per cent.
The statement goes on to express the opinion that the
work of the white labourer should be confined to the
skilled departments.

But the Special Commissioner of the *Pall Mall
Gazette*, writing from Capetown, puts the matter in
even stronger form. He says: ' Until he [the native]
' has been induced to work it would be folly to suppose
' that the time has come for wholesale and indiscrimi-
' nate emigration of skilled artisans from England to
' South Africa. Without an unlimited supply of un-
' skilled labour the demand for skilled labour must
' necessarily be proportionately limited. There are those
' who would endeavour to replace black unskilled labour
' by white. What does this mean? We should want
' something like three-quarters of a million of white
' labourers for this purpose at the present day. With
' their families we may take it that they would repre-
' sent some three millions of white people imported into
' the country. Where are they to come from? Who
' is going to bring them over? And, above all, who is
' going to feed them when they get here? The answer
' to the first of these is "Not from England," and to
' the last two "Nobody." To live in South Africa an
' Englishman always requires nearly twice as much
' money as he does at home, and in some parts of the
' country at least three times as much. If white un-
' skilled labourers were to take over the work of the
' Kafir, the white men would either have to do so for
' about the rate of wages now paid to Kafirs—say,
' 2*l*. 10*s*. per month on the mines—or to allow all the
' important industries in South Africa to close. The
' fallacy of the argument used by the *Times* in ad-
' vocating white unskilled labour for the Rand is best
' illustrated by the fact that, if that principle were to be
' carried out, and the white labourer received a white
' man's wage, the whole of the gold output would be

' insufficient to meet the weekly pay-sheet. The sum
' is a simple one. To turn out 15,000,000*l.* worth of
' gold in a year about 150,000 men are required. Of
' these about 125,000 would be unskilled. At the very
' lowest computation their wage would be 8*s.* a day.
' Then there would be 25,000 skilled men, averaging at
' least 16*s.* per day. Taking only 300 working days to
' the year, and that is under the mark, the men's wages
' would amount to 21,000,000*l.*, which, without allow-
' ing anything for plant, materials, and ordinary trade
' expenses, would show an annual deficit of 6,000,000*l.*
' The larger the number of mines open the greater the
' loss would be. And what applies so forcibly to gold
' mining applies even more convincingly to the other
' and less favoured industries of this country. Every-
' thing would be ruined. I point all this out to make it
' clear that, however much we may enjoy rolling that
' pleasing platitude, " a white man's country," round
' our tongue, South Africa is not, and never can be, a
' country for the unskilled white labourer. If we persist
' in forcing unskilled white labour upon South Africa
' we shall merely be degrading the white man to the
' level of the Kafir. One of the worst features of this is
' that he will never be able to support a white wife and
' family. Then he will become, as many have already,
' a Kafir in his methods of life. In time he will become
' the father of a coloured family. His children may or
' may not be useful to him, but they can never be an
' acquisition to the community.'

Seeing that the mines have done and are now
doing their best to acquire the most modern labour-
saving machinery, and that the wholesale employment
of white raw labour is out of the question on the score

of expense, the question as presented to-day is narrowed down to a native or Asiatic supply. It may be stated, parenthetically, that this barrier to the employment of European labour to the same extent as in Australia and America is mainly, if not solely, due to the fact that South Africa is not self-supporting in its food supply, and is dependent upon distant regions for its necessaries of life. Flour is brought from Australia ; mealies from South America; meat from both these regions; while such daily condiments as butter, jam, bacon, onions, and eggs are all imported from outside. That such should be the case in an essentially pastoral land is, as previously pointed out, more due to the lack of industry of the Boer and the native, the classes which take the place of agriculturists elsewhere, than due to the poorness of the soil or the occasional evils of drought and cattle sickness. This parlous condition may be capable of modification, and when beef, mutton, and flour approximate to the prices current in Australia and the States, perhaps the European labourer may be imported to work at a wage more favourable to his chances of competition with the native than he has to-day.

The relation that native labour has to mining is seen in the numbers employed and the monthly wage bill. Before the war, in 1899, the number employed (August) was 96,704, which at an average wage of 50s. per head amounted to some 240,000l. per month. The later statistics subsequent to peace being declared show the number of natives dwindling to 68,000 (August, 1903), and the wage bill reduced, taken at the same rate, to 170,000l., which reduction in wage bill not only affects the mines, but also local commerce—a

difference of some 84,000*l.* per annum. The number
of natives at work is slowly increasing, it is true (for
August month a net increase of 1,566), but at the
present rate of increase the total required for the
growing expansion of the industry and for other
developments, such as for railways and agriculture, will
have little chance of being reached within measurable
time. In fact, the demand grows with accumulative
force, and will continue to grow until some solution is
found for its satisfaction, or until the South African
colonies reach that phase where industrial progress is
slow, proceeding more from internal consolidation than
external growth.

The retardation of industry by the lack of labour
is not only having immediate effect, but is deferring
activity in the near and distant future to the absolute
detriment of the country. The argument that to spin
out a limitable industry, such as gold mining, does
little or no harm, in that only the amount of ore available can in any case be mined, cannot stand examination. More especially is the argument a weak one
where the industry is the life of the country. Gold
mining in South Africa is the foundation and soil from
which all other industries spring. If the ground be
impoverished by a spreading out of the fertilising
medium to an insufficient depth and in insufficient
quantities, the fruits will be poor and scanty and lack
permanence. The deeper the soil the better the root
and the more fruitful the tree. Colonists look forward
to the time when, fed by a good gold yield, agriculture
and industry will flourish and become permanent
sources of national wealth. Due to growing revenue
and generous surpluses irrigation will be undertaken,

ports will develop, and manufactures be established. With a limited and restricted gold industry these possibilities will vanish, and the country will be deprived of its potential means of development. Quoting concrete cases, in a review of deep levels which appeared in the *African Review* of January 31, 1903, it was shown in the case of the South Nourse Company that the equipment of the property is laid out on the basis of 200 stamps, but it is ' the intention at the beginning only ' to erect 100 stamps and to start reduction operations ' as soon as the mine development is sufficiently ad- ' vanced to keep these supplied with ore. Shaft sink- ' ing was commenced on June 9, 1899, and at the time ' of the suspension of active operations in October of ' that year the shafts had reached depths of 70 and ' 77 feet respectively. Since the resumption of the ' equipment operations, no shaft sinking has been ' carried on, as only a very small staff of labourers has ' been obtainable, and the few men employed are en- ' gaged in surface construction work. So soon as the ' necessary labour is available, the sinking of the shafts ' will be continued; the reefs should be intersected in ' about $2\frac{1}{2}$ years. Reduction operations should com- ' mence in about two years from then, so that the first ' gold will probably be produced in about $4\frac{1}{2}$ years after ' the necessary labour becomes available.'

Should the ' necessary labour ' not be available this period of activity will be deferred proportionately, to the detriment of the present and future inhabitant and to the loss of the present shareholder; for capital in abundance is there, the sum provided having been 523,908*l.*, of which some 100,000*l.* has been spent, and the balance was available   This means in the case of one deep level a sum of over 400,000*l*. awaiting expenditure. In the case of the Jumpers Deep the following table shows its past record :

Period	Ore milled	Gold produced	Average Cost per Ton of Ore milled			Total Value of Gold produced	Average Value per Ton of Ore milled			Profit	Profit per Ton of Ore milled		
	Tons	Oz.	£	s.	d.	£	£	s.	d.	£	£	s.	d.
First year (7 months) ending September 30, 1898	82,245	43 895	1	13	6	184,413	2	4	10	46,369	0	11	3
Second year to war, October, 1899 ..	177,092	89,026	1	8	9	372,446	2	2	1	117,394	0	13	3
Third year (8 months) ending September 30, 1902	74,119	26,115	1	5	7	109,152	1	9	5	14,061	0	3	9
Totals and averages	333,456	159,036	1	9	3	666,012	1	19	11	177,825	0	10	8

NOTE.—The expenditure and revenue from the closing down of mine in October, 1899, to recommencement of milling on February 2, 1902, are not included in the above.

From these figures it is seen that the mine was getting into good profit-earning condition before the war. The position since the war has been abnormal. A factor which prompted the directors in pursuing the policy of only keeping things going since they received their complement of 750 natives was that they did not wish to encroach too much upon the ore reserves in the mine. With plenty of labour this mine would rapidly become a fine paying proposition, distributing work and dividends to British citizens while a customer to British industries. Without labour the property languishes and contributes its portion to the prevailing atrophy. At a meeting of the Jupiter Gold Mining Company, held at London about the same period, the

Chairman was detailing how that Company has some 705,000*l.* for mining development in its coffers, 'a fact ' which only renders the more regrettable the impossi- ' bility of employing for the present the large sums now ' available for the purpose for which they have been got ' together—that is to say, the development and equip- ' ment of the Company's property. It is precisely this ' compulsory postponement of the time when share- ' holders should expect to be obtaining a due return on ' the money they have subscribed, which brings home ' to us most forcibly the vital importance to the whole ' industry of securing an adequate supply of labour.'

Mr. C. T. Goldmann, a well-known authority on mining and the statistics of the industry, says in a letter to the *Times*, dated March 23 :

' The further development of the mines should, it ' is calculated, increase the stamps at work within five ' years from 6,500 to 17,000 ; and as the number of ' white and black labourers for every 100 stamps crush- ' ing is approximately 175 and 1,300 respectively, the ' additional requirements will, within that period, amount ' to 18,000 white skilled labourers and 135,000 natives, ' exclusive of the needs of those ventures that are ' then in a preparatory stage. Add thereto the con- ' current increasing demand in all branches of trade, ' from the impetus resulting from the construction ' of railways and other public works and industrial ' and domestic requirements, and from these some ' conception may be formed of the magnitude and ' difficulties of the question.' It is consequently seen by this estimate that the absence of these 135,000 unskilled labourers would spell some 18,000 white men being deprived of the opportunity of employment in the colony, greatly to their own and their country's detriment.

Mr. Hennen Jennings, in his presidential address to the members of the Institution of Mining and Metallurgy of London, speaking of the Witwatersrand fields remarked, that as regards the future there is little left to man but a small margin to improve upon in the department of percentage of extraction. 'The ' crux of the present position is this : At what cost can ' the gold be extracted, and in what time ? As working ' costs are reduced, so will more and more of the con-' glomerate beds warrant exploitation. The quicker and ' greater the returns the more justification is there for ' the capitalist to put up great sums of money for the ' development and exploitation of the fields. In the ' sphere of working costs the dominant factor is labour. ' Probably this factor has never been found in a more ' intricate or complex setting.' The *South African Mines*, a journal published in Johannesburg, puts the number of additional stamps to be erected in the next five years, if all goes well, at 8,000, bringing the total to 14,500 stamps in 1908. On the basis of former requirements, this will mean an importation of 12,800,000l. worth of machinery ; or, with additional requirements of shafts, coal mines, other non-producing mines, &c., the estimate is raised to 17,000,000l., while the weight of material—500,000 tons—materially concerns railway prosperity.

Put in another form, the mines of the Rand being divided into two classes, the producing and the developing or non-producing properties, the coloured labour available was distributed in the beginning of this year thus :

—	Producing Mines	Non-Producing Mines	Total
January . . .	31,796	7,224	39,020
February . . .	33,570	8,760	42,330
March . . .	37,354	9,522	46,876
April . . .	39,085	10,735	49,820

The average number of natives apportioned to the non-producing properties per month from the total secured was 900, and this moiety of labour, so necessary for development, was granted by the distributing agency of the Chamber of Mines at the sacrifice of the producing properties. It is estimated that these 900 boys drafted to developing mines would permit, if labour were more plentiful, of the running of 75 extra stamps per month, with the corresponding white employment, expenditure, profit, and gold output.

The position, we think, is clear that native labour or coloured and cheap labour of some sort is not only essential for the Rand mines, but is almost equally important for each South African state, and is of considerable importance to the British manufacturer and British financier who benefit by the gold extracted from the mines in proportion of cost and profit; for of the gold won that portion which is absorbed by the cost of working—in wages and material—is accounted for in living, clothing, tools, and machinery, while that portion which is profit and falls to the share of the capitalist and the shareholder becomes circulated in greater part in the luxuries of the rich.

It has already been demonstrated that, under the present conditions of native temperament; under existing life, customs, predilection and environment of the

tribal races; providing the native population as estimated
be approximately correct, there is but a small chance
in the near future for the supply to expand to anything
approaching the growth of the demand. We speak
as far as the races south of the Zambesi are concerned.
North of that division, in the vast interior of Africa,
from coast to coast and to the Soudan, many millions
of blacks subsist in different grades of civilisation or
savagery, yet each sphere of European influence has
its own labour troubles despite the native hordes.
Uganda, Somaliland, West Africa, Congo Free State,
British Central Africa Protectorate, Barotseland, and
other adjacent regions have been tried by the several
labour agencies, none up to the present yielding any
degree of satisfaction.   It is therefore scarcely surprising
that the heads of the crippled mining industry, who
have their responsibilities with their dividends, and who
cannot, did they so desire, divest themselves of the one
and retain the other, have for some period had their
attention directed to other sources of labour presenting
less difficulty in supply and negotiation. The first
impulse, especially at this period of anxious desire to
promote British emigration, was to reconsider matters
and strive to fill the void with the British working
man.   Steps were taken to give wider employment to
the whites, to the extent that the relative proportion
of white worker and native worker has already been
reduced from one to eight to one to five.   But when
the attempt was made to fill even a portion of the
actual sphere of the native with the European it
brought failure.   Five shillings a day was the sum
offered, being more than double the wage of the native
worker and a half to a third less than the skilled

white miner. The result was that the unskilled
European was found unequal to two skilled natives,
while the wage he earned was not even a bare pittance.
Even if the mining magnates and managers discarded
all business principles and turned philanthropists and
self-sacrificing patriots, determining to employ British
workmen instead of blacks, a solution is no nearer,
for the payment of a fair wage measured by the cost
of Rand living would entail the closing down of the
lower-grade mines and the abandonment of all deep-
level sinking, the enhanced cost demanding inordinate
capital expenditure. The natives also, in such case,
would be thrown out of their employment; for to merely
supplement raw native labour by placing raw white
labour at a higher wage side by side with the nigger
would scarcely be practicable with due regard to caste,
and would also breed dissatisfaction among the lower-
paid black workers.

As throwing a side-light on these efforts to employ
unskilled white labour, quite recently the Cape Government negotiated for the immigration and employment
of Italian labourers; their proposals were rejected by
the representative of the Italian Government upon
examination on the score that the proffered wage
offered no inducement to the immigrant.

South African sources proving insufficient, Central,
North, and West African proving impracticable, Europeans impossible under the prevailing cost of living,
the leaders of Rand mining turned their attention to
Indians and Chinese. Indian coolies, though considered physically fit and otherwise willing and desirable, yet found little favour for the peculiar and
apparently illogical reason that they were British

subjects. Being British subjects the insuperable difficulty of enforced repatriation at end of service stood
as an obstacle to their employment, and legislation has
already been passed restricting their further increase in
the land owing to the pressure they exert against the
small European trader. The Chinese proposition
alone remains as providing a means by which an
unlimited number of labourers may be engaged from
an exhaustless source, and at the same time to be had
under defined conditions of exclusive employment at
the mines with an engagement to leave at end of
service. Despite the strong opposition against the
employment and immigration of Chinamen, those responsible for the progress of the mines can see no
other alternative.

Without adopting any assumption that Chinese
labour is easily procurable and will be found to serve
the purpose—as these essential conditions are still
under investigation—one may examine the principle
and seek to analyse those doubts and objections with
which the proposition has been greeted. The protests
may be dealt with under three heads—immorality,
invasion of European sphere of industry, risk of importing a new factor into the colour problem. As regards
the charge of immorality, brought specifically against
the Chinaman, authorities widely differ. Employers of
Chinese coolies speak in praise of their honesty, their
cleanliness, and deem them no more or less immoral
than other races. Others declare that the Chinese
coolie imports many strange vices into the regions he
penetrates. Under the provisions of the law which it
is proposed to impose in this connection, the Chinese
labourer would be segregated at least to an extent to

confine his mode of living to the compound of his habitation. There would be no free intercourse with the races of his environment. Consequently, his effect upon his surroundings would be so minimised, however evil he may be—and we do not admit that the Chinee is more evil as a being than another—that his influence in the social system would be ineffective. With regard to invading the sphere of European activity, as the hired immigrant would be imported for one specific purpose and would not be permitted to embark in any other vocation, and as a check upon this every Chinee in the country could be registered and require a passport, we see no fear of such an evil resulting. As a matter of fact, many Chinese have for some time in the past been established in South Africa in diverse vocations, their descendants by coloured women reinforcing the mixed race commonly known as the Cape Boy—an industrious and capable class.

Shorn of all subordinate factors, such as opposition from the neighbouring States; the natural distrust engendered by the adoption of a principle which has elsewhere, but under different conditions, proved disastrous; the benefits of such a departure to the mining industry, on whose behalf the scheme is projected, are patent. In lieu of an unstable source of labour supply governed by conditions over which the employer has no control, a successful system of coolie importation would remove the most formidable obstacle to the progress of the mining industry. The supply could always be regulated by the demand, and if through the adoption of suitable measures sufficient native labour be in the future available, contracts with the

imported article need not be renewed, and a rehabilita-
tion of the native can take place without any serious
dislocation of mining work. Instead of the natives
being the masters of the situation, they would be
relegated to their proper sphere as clients for work and
not the arbiters. The native would have a competitor,
and would be willing to accept the value of his hire
and not as hitherto the value he sets on his hire. The
presence of Chinese would create a sort of emulation
among them, influencing them to strive to become as
expert as their yellow brethren. There is nothing to
indicate any weakness in the native's temperament
causing him to sink into extinction under the burden of
idleness and incapacity induced by severe competition.
In the Cape Colony he competes strongly with the
Cape half-caste, the Malay, the coolie, and the poor
white. In Natal he farms, acts as policeman, does
the navvying, and fills most of the minor posts in
the workshop. The Indian coolie is in a similar
position in Natal as Chinese unrestricted importation
would cause the Chinaman to be in in the Transvaal—
he would neither displace nor oust the native from any
sphere, but, on the contrary, rather tend to make him
more industrially aggressive. As an effect on the
native Chinese immigration would do more good than
harm. As elsewhere stated, outside the sphere of
mining are numerous occupations open to the industrious native. Farm and house work, stables, road
making, railways and numerous other avenues of employment are available should he alter his ways and
become less lazy. The knowledge that only by labour
can he obtain the wherewithal to purchase the luxuries
which his betters enjoy will have a slow but certain

effect if left to time; but the mines can't wait for this natural consummation. The Kafir will learn much from the Chinese—and pay for it. The knowledge gained will not probably be strong from an ethical standpoint, but a little worldly ambition to displace the slovenly fatalism of the raw African native will not come amiss. Doubtless were the native alive to his own interest he would turn to and embrace the offer to work for a liberal wage at his own doorstep; but as he declines to voluntarily apply, and his education is a matter of time, there appears no other alternative for the strenuous European but to take steps which, though not altogether to his liking, will yet be productive of relief in the most important direction, in fact that direction alone which induces him to stay and make the land his home.

Mr. George Albu, speaking at Johannesburg on February 26, at the annual general meeting of the Meyer and Charlton Company, thus referred to the Chinese labour proposals :

'There is no one in Johannesburg who desires more 'keenly than myself to keep this a white man's country, 'and I believe that the fears expressed if Chinese 'labour is even temporarily employed are greatly 'exaggerated. In a few years' time the Transvaal 'will have to bear the heavy burden of providing 'the interest charge on the loans of 65,000,000*l.* 'which are to be raised for industrial purposes and 'the contribution towards the expenditure of Great 'Britain on the war. It cannot do this unless the 'mining industry prospers, because it is from that 'industry the largest portion of the revenue must 'necessarily come. . . I would commence by importing, 'say, 10,000 Chinese and employing them exclusively

'at deep-level mines, as an experiment. The enemies
' of the yellow race will cry out that the Chinaman does
' not make a good citizen, and drains the country of
' the money he earns. But you have to face the alter-
' native. Are you content to leave buried in the ground
' for an indefinite period, gold to the value of hundreds
' of millions sterling, and stunt the growth of South
' Africa because you begrudge a few hundred thousands
' of that wealth dribbling away to another country?
' You might as well adopt the attitude that you will
' not work the mines because some of the gold won
' goes to Germany and America for the purchase of
' machinery and other supplies. Look on the other
' side of the picture. If the labour complement were
' added to by 50,000, it would set South Africa aflame
' with prosperity. In a short time the mines would
' employ nearly double the number of skilled white
' men at present engaged. Trade would revive by
' leaps and bounds, and natives would be liberated for
' the agricultural development of the country districts.
' Thereby the mealies, for instance, which we are now
' compelled to import, could be grown in the country,
' and the tendency would be to effect that very reform
' upon which the future so much depends, cheaper cost
' of living.'

Whether Chinese be found suitable and willing, or
whether the Indian coolie be the final selection, it is
certain that labour from some permanent and perennial supply is the great need in the Rand. In a discussion on native labour at a Chamber of Mines meeting
held last May, Sir Percy Fitzpatrick adequately
described the position when he expressed his fears that
should the Government trench upon the native labour

supply for their public works requirements, seeing that railways alone were estimated to require at least 10,000 'boys,' and, perhaps, 40,000, it would make the importation of cheap coloured labourers from somewhere absolutely necessary. If the Government imported the labour necessary for these works it would, besides relieving the strain, obtain at a small cost convincing proof as to whether legislative safeguards could be effective for the regulation of imported labour. The substitution of unskilled white labour for native labour was an economic impossibility. He favoured the view that considerable portions of the railway work should be done by whites, but he strongly deprecated bringing into the country a large force of unskilled whites, who would be thrown on the community at the end of their term without work, a situation being thus brought about which would force heartless competition with the present workers and cause great distress. Continuing, Sir Percy Fitzpatrick said that all Africa was based upon cheap coloured labour. It not only set the pace, but fixed the limit of accomplishment, and unless this factor was obtainable far more plentifully than at present it would be necessary to revise the estimates that had been made as to the possibilities of the industry, and that might mean, indeed, the establishment of a position similar to that in Western Australia, where they had the greatest goldfield in the world, but no labour to work it. On the mining industry of the Transvaal an immense superstructure was raised— social, commercial, industrial, and political—and it was eminently desirable that every obstacle to its expansion should be removed. Imported labour was required for the railways, and he urged the mining industry and the whole community to say so boldly. It was quite clear to him that the industry could not give away any native labour without forcing the question of importing Asiatics into immediate prominence.

Having endeavoured to show the absolute necessity for South Africa of labour for the mines, the benefits derivable by the many from the gold produced, the legitimacy of the demand, and the obstacles to the employment of white labour as an alternative, we will now proceed to consider the present method of native employment and strive to indicate where it fails so as to necessitate recourse to Chinese, and suggest a policy tending to improvement. Since the fame of the Kimberley Diamond Fields as a money-distributing centre first permeated the native peoples it has been the custom of 'boys' to trek to the mines in gradually increasing quantities and from gradually increasing distances. Shangaans from the East Coast and boys from the banks of the Zambesi wended their way to Kimberley across hundreds of miles of intervening and strange countries for the sake of earning *igold*, or *maali*, with but little if any extraneous inducement or pressure. Naturally the Basuto, the Bechuana, and the Transvaal native, being nearer, were the first to take this pilgrimage. Throughout these years of native employment there never has been any system in vogue which by the utmost stretch of imagination could be legitimately termed slavery or even forced labour, despite the persistent accusations so freely hurled at the miner and the colonist by people at home. The only method which might give colour to this charge was in the case of natives being recruited for labour direct from the chiefs. This practice of direct enlistment sprang from the jealousy and the greed of the chiefs at seeing their men freely departing, some returning with comparative wealth, and others never returning. In either case the chief was concerned, for wealth in the hands of a subject without the chief having a finger in the pie was *infra dig.*, affected his authority, and did not satisfy his avarice; when the native wanderer failed to return the chief lost a subject. So it soon became a custom (and served the needs of both parties to the contract) for labour touts to deal direct with the chief and obtain from him a certain number of ' boys,' for which concession the chief got well paid, while the natives engaged were unaffected in that they also obtained their customary wage. This method had the advantage of conciliating and satisfying the chief, while vesting the labour agent with some authority over his ' boys.' But these ' boys ' were in no sense ' slaves,' either to the chief or to their white employer; on the contrary, the chief in most cases declined to use more than ordinary persuasion or grant his permission for the ' boys ' to enlist. The bargain generally had to be arranged with the individual, and when the boy arrived at his place of employment he in no wise felt himself bound to work for the employer who had conveyed him there, very often deserting, especially if his treatment was not kind and honest. Another method in vogue, both in the early diamond fields and later at Barberton and Johannesburg, was that of ' touting '; a ' tout ' being an agent who may be termed a freelance, in that he collected stray natives and brought them to the places of demand and sold them to employers at a certain sum per head by way of commission, just as a labour bureau might do in England. This also made no difference to the native, for he only engaged himself when the prevailing wage was agreed upon, and then, if the work or the master did not please him, incontinently shifted his quarters, sometimes just to the next compound, and at other times to some adjacent mining district. A proper system of check against the desertions has never yet been invented in mining circles, for to the ordinary man one black face was like another, and ' boy ' ' Jim ' became ' boy ' ' Sixpence ' in the most informal manner. Even the prevailing and existing Pass Law was little help; for a ' boy's ' pass was transferred as lightly as may be from the one ' boy ' to another with but little compunction or fear of detection. Certainly some compound managers and detectives are keener than others, and occasionally the deserter or deserters were traced and punished, but the proportion of detections to the whole has always been too insignificant to count for anything more than a fluke. Not only are natives thus apt to shift quarters at the smallest provocation or caprice, but a large portion of the native ' workers ' amid a European community take a holiday for a term without leave, or after their term of engagement has expired, and spend their time in easy travel among their friends in service, eating the masters' and mistresses' food, and enjoying free lodgings without detection. Each boy has his ' friend ' or ' friends,' or ' brothers,' as they are variously termed, and it is always difficult for an employer to distinguish between his Kafir's casual acquaintance (of which it is difficult to deprive him, and sometimes dangerous, for fear of desertion) and the professional loafer. This evil of ' friends ' has to a large extent been coped with by periodical raids by the police on locations and compounds in search of passless ' boys,' or those with passes out of date and not renewed. But it would be a clever police officer indeed who would manage to eliminate even approximately this well-known social evil from the towns of South Africa.

As showing how in cases this working in the mines for what must be termed a generous wage to the simple native operates, Mr. George Griffiths, writing to the *Sussex Daily News* on the subject, recalls a circumstance when he was at Kimberley and visited the De Beers compound, of a grizzled old Basuto who had no less than 700*l.* to his credit in the books of the firm. He had prudently not tasted any strong drink but Kafir beer for years ; he was free to leave at the end of any one of the three months' contracts which he signed. Sometimes he took three months' leave and went back to his people, but for some fifteen years he always came back to the compound to make his pile a little bigger. ' This,' remarks Mr. Griffiths, ' is only one of many similar results which this miscalled system of slavery produces.'

But still more striking testimony to the possibility of natives who receive the normal wage accumulating respectable sums is provided in a case which came before the Magistrate's Court at Johannesburg recently. It appears, as reported in the *Rand Daily Mail*, that in October, 1899, one Kambani lived in Buxton Street, Doornfontein, and, not being a spendthrift, saved all the money he possibly could, intending, when funds permitted, to retire into the country and purchase a wife. He had amassed the respectable sum of 298*l.*, but decided to work a little longer ere he sought pastures new. Unfortunately, however, war broke out, and this was the cause of an alteration in Kambani's programme. He had two friends to whom he was unwise enough to entrust his money, with the result that he never saw it again. In the course of evidence against one of the accused, who was subsequently arrested, the Rev. Bailey Shaw, of St. Cyprian's, Brickfields, stated that he knew the accused for some time. At either the end of 1899 or the beginning of 1900, he came to witness and asked him to mind some money (about 280*l*.). Witness asked him how he became possessed of so large a sum, and accused said he kept ' a native curio shop.' Witness questioned him further, and finally refused to mind the money. This conclusively proved that the sum claimed was in the possession of these natives. Bearing upon the same theme, denoting how easy it is for the South African native to earn money for his wants, and more than his wants, is an incident which occurred recently in Rhodesia. A farmer caught a number of native women cutting wood on his farm, and when asked the reason they replied that their husbands had sent them to cut wood and sell it in town, as the hut-tax had to be paid next month. When asked why their husbands did not go out to work and earn the money, the native women replied that their husbands did not work.

From these circumstances it is easy to gather that the native in South Africa has a very easy time of it, has the means of accumulating quite a respectable sum, and that when in employment his movements are free, or only restricted by the limits of his pass, restrictions easily evaded ; that he is never kept a day longer in employment than his wishes dictate, and that the native population of all towns is much in excess of actual employment ; not because there is not work enough, but because a large proportion prefer to take a holiday to working ; living in idleness on their ' brothers ' and European employers. This may be said to be the bright side of native life, and judged by their hilarious chatterings whenever natives do congregate they are very pleased with themselves, and almost die with laughter at the smart way they circumvent the beastly energetic Englishman. But the life of a native amid European surroundings has its seamy side, and though a native is not much given to moroseness or fretting, yet from his own point of view much sacrifice is suffered when he leaves his home to dwell among the white men. Undoubtedly they miss the free life and congenial companionship of the kraal. They leave their womenkind behind, miss their faction fights, their pagan rites, their witch-doctors and their periodical carouse and palavers. A native, in common with other carnivora, delights in killing his meat and devouring it at his will. He enjoys a bask by the river and sometimes a dip. He sighs for his delicate pumpkin tops and other veld edibles unobtainable in the towns, and loves to discuss local doings and happenings at the chief's kraal. Whilst in service, it is true, he sleeps under a watertight roof, has more regular food, is safe from slaughter or harm, waxes fat on plenty of porridge, and has the means to purchase any little luxury he may fancy ; but against these advantages he misses his kraal dances, his laughter and play in the moonlight, his tramp across the veld, his happy and indolent life, his dogs and his cattle. It is therefore seen that from a material side,

though he is better off in employment, he suffers from
that lack of contact with natural surroundings which
with us is called home sickness. We think that very
much more might be done than is attempted to-day to
reconcile the raw native to his novel surroundings, not
that efforts are not being made in this direction. As
announced by Sir Percy Fitzpatrick at the last annual
meeting of the Rand Mines at Johannesburg, ' Many
' small improvements have been made during the year,
' adding to the comfort and health, and, of course,
' eventually to the efficiency of the natives. Drying-
' rooms, steam-heated, have been erected next to the
' shafts on most of the subsidiaries, and are being erected
' on the others. In these rooms natives are able to
' shelter before going down the mine and after coming
' out, if they can be persuaded to do so ; but they seem
' to prefer, regardless of weather, getting back to the
' compounds at once, and rather than force them to pass
' through the drying-room, we are now considering the
' advisability of building a covered way from the shaft
' into the compound ; for it is clear to us that pneumonia
' and other pulmonary complaints responsible for a
' large proportion of sickness amongst natives must
' arise from this period of exposure, when the native
' comes up hot out of the shaft and in his light calico
' clothing dawdles about the surface before going to his
' quarters. We are also discussing the possibility of
' issuing at cost price some article of clothing like a long
' warm smock, which the natives would be compelled to
' wear on coming out of the mine as a protection against
' cold. In the drying-rooms we have hot coffee and hot
' soup, a ration of which is issued to each of the natives
' before his shift.'

With regard to diet, Sir Percy said it was decided several months ago 'to make an attempt to do their ' own gardening and provide their own vegetables for ' the staff. The area of land set aside for these gardens ' is 37⅓ acres. About half of the produce has been ' consumed, and the following had been distributed up ' to date : Green mealies, 41,300 ; potatoes, 31,973 lb. ; ' pumpkins, 5,074 ; turnips, 798 lb. : vegetable marrows, ' 6,157 lb. ; other vegetables, 3,500 lb. The amount spent ' upon this, including fencing, &c., was 2,021*l*. 7*s*. 1*d*.' Praiseworthy as these endeavours to safeguard the health and welfare of the native *employé* must be deemed, yet they tend more to alleviate the body than the spirit; to make the native lot bearable rather than attractive.

In the words of Mr. F. G. Elliott, Inspector of Native Compounds, Rhodesia : 'At the Globe and ' Phœnix. . . . one of the new rooms, 120 feet by 15 ' feet, in this compound was fitted with wooden bunks ' in tiers of three, to hold 160 men in all ; but so large ' a number could not be expected to crowd into an ' apartment which afforded insufficient space for more ' than sixty men ! At present half the natives on the ' mine prefer to live in grass and pole huts outside the ' enclosure.' And the same applies to the towns. A similar story is told by Mr. Walton, M.L.A., of the Cape. In a debate in the House on the Native Locations Act as in operation at Port Elizabeth, the leading Cape port, he said :

'At Port Elizabeth the native objected to an order ' of things by which he became a monthly or yearly ' tenant. Some of the natives belonged to the floating ' section of the population ; but others were permanent

' inhabitants, and the last-mentioned objected to a
' system of tenure under which they would be unable to
' make proper provision for their wives and families.
' Some means should be devised of giving the native
' that reasonable tenure for his house which he wanted,
' and without which, the speaker was afraid, he would
' continue to resist any endeavours to put him into
' these locations. Although a location had been opened
' at Port Elizabeth since the first of the month, and a
' special officer sent thither by the Government—a most
' tactful man—yet the great majority of the natives
' absolutely refused to go into these locations. The
' native was now purchasing little plots of ground just
' outside the municipality, on which he erected his
' shanty or little cottage. He believed 40,000*l.* had
' been spent on the construction of the dwellings ; only
' a comparatively small number of them were being let ;
' whereas a large location was growing up on the out-
' skirts of the town.' Measures are demanded to fit
the surroundings of the native worker in better accord
with the life he is accustomed to. Some suggestions
to this end we will now endeavour to outline.

CHAPTER X

TREATMENT OF MINING NATIVES

As may be gathered by that which has already been said, the shortfall of labour on the mines is not only due to lack of numbers seeking work, but also to the short terms of service of those engaged. An employer considers himself exceptionally lucky if in a batch of new *employés* the average service per ' boy ' be six months. The monthly desertions and departures in normal times nearly equal the arrivals and very often exceed their number. As may be appreciated, a journey which takes anything from a week to a month (in earlier times before the railways were built the journey undertaken by the greater portion of the natives to reach the mines took sometimes two months or more) in both coming and returning made a big hole in the year's absence. If a native were to work steadily for a term of years not only would he become a proficient miner but also his period of service would be proportionately extended to the sum of saving the time wasted on an annual trip and an extended holiday. Also many who leave the gold mines after a few months' service never have the desire to return, naturally preferring the life of ease at the kraal to the regular labour in the mine. Whatever predilections they might have had for civilised customs and regular life soon vanish when put to the test of native surroundings. If the choice were simply one between agricultural labour and pastoral life or mining labour and town or compound life, then the selection of the agrarian surroundings would be a worthy one and open to no criticism. An agricultural producer is at least as worthy as a town worker. But such an alternative does not offer. It is in most cases either mining or town labour or kraal and a life of indolence. In farming, the alternative is either agricultural labour under the European, or a pastoral life of hand-to-mouth ease, a round of plenty, famine, carouse, brawl, and dirt, in mixed proportions. To be said in favour of kraal life is the simplicity of thought, living and energy, freedom of action and liberty to saunter, stroll, or lie at ease without a thought of the day that follows. An ideal of the Utopian, but not of the strenuous. If the African native were superfluous in the economy of the European doubtless his ideal would not be disturbed, and he would either disappear gradually from the land that knew him or his increase would pile up until he became a burden and a nightmare to his Government and country, entailing drastic measures when the pressure became serious. But the conditions in South Africa are such that the native is wanted; he has his niche in the polity of the state, and his sphere in industry. Not being a wealthy class nor a cultured class, but occupying the position of the proletariat in other countries, Kafirs have either to labour or be preserved in idleness. At present the native is merely dallying with his work. It is not so much need as curiosity and ambition which lead him to the labour market. Labour with him is an episode and not a recognised lot in life. It is for the

employer to convert this episode into a natural necessity,
and the best means to this end is to familiarise him
with civilised conditions and encourage him to a more
settled life. Five months' labour and twelve months'
ease are not calculated to arouse habits of industry. It
is to the interest of the employer, and we speak here
specifically of the mining employer, to induce the
native to stay longer and take more interest in his
work. It is at least as important for each native to
work twelve months instead of six as it is to obtain
two natives to work twelve months between them. But
the present method in vogue, with all the care for his
health and well-being, is entirely unfitted to bring about
this result. It is entirely based on a temporary lodging
principle and offers no inducement for a permanency.
The mines have their model cottages for the European
miner, but no model kraals for the native. The native
labourer comes raw from the veld and his accustomed
life at the kraal to the ugliest of surroundings and the
minimum of comfort. He misses his wife, his *intombi*,
his family circle, his cattle, his goats and his sheep.
Though not possible within the limits of mining surroundings to give him all he is accustomed to in his own
native district, yet much might be done to make his
lot less of a break from his accustomed life than it is
on the Rand. Instead of the barrack-like compound
there might be a kraal-like barracks. Large native,
and perhaps tribal, reserves within the vicinity of the
Rand might be substituted for the close, crowded, and
confined compounds near the shaft; men might be
encouraged to emigrate to the gold mines with their
families, young men to have wives, to keep a few goats
and fowls and possibly cattle; a few acres for cultiva-

tion or market gardening, tobacco growing, and other reliefs from mining work. In short, in order to induce a permanent nucleus of mining labour, endeavour to establish a community of miners in the vicinity of the mines on the same lines upon which the European mines are worked. Johannesburg, it is true, has its coloured location; but not its native village. The coloured quarters of the Rand are dens of vice and dirt; mixture and admixture; bastard, Kafir, and Hottentot— not at all alluring to the raw native fresh from the kraal. The surface surroundings of the Rand are not so valuable as to forbid a number of large and small native villages, patrolled and superintended by policemen and reserved for workers. Churches and schools might be erected, habits of cleanliness enforced, stores and savings banks established, providing the link between civilisation and savagery. Railways or tramways for the conveyance of the labourers to the mine and back would not be too expensive an undertaking, the trade and the traffic between the location and the town and mines probably covering the working expenses. The result of such a movement would without doubt justify its adoption. Loafers and idlers would be rigorously excluded, to the extent of not permitting a non-worker, other than a member of the family, whether male or female, to remain in the location for a longer period than, say, two days.

Such a scheme of native settlement need not necessarily be undertaken in its fulness at once. A settlement of this description might be started close to one of the lines of rails radiating from Johannesburg with a few selected 'boys' of approved conduct; a few families located in their midst, such as native

policemen's families and those boys engaged on the
mines who are already mated locally. If proper dwellings were built the applicants for transference from the
compound to the kraal would be numerous enough.
The system of accommodation might be a compromise
between the conventional compound and the native *kia*,
such as square or round habitations of non-inflammable
building material used in portable bungalows, with
every three or four huts a separate *segothla* or enclosure.
The settlement would partake of the model lodging
principle applied to natives, a Garden City,[1] with a
common recreation ground, with trees and shade, a place
for bathing—either derived from a natural watercourse
or artificially constructed—a common fuel supply, and
all the inexpensive conveniences to make the life of the
inhabitant at least as comfortable as by his native
hearth. The problem of the women would be solved
in the many avenues open to native women in the
vicinity in laundries and domestic service, while even
the wives might find employment at the mines on surface work ; many of the native women would desire to
supplement the earnings of the male. *Piccaninns* are
always in demand in and around Johannesburg. But
it is not suggested that all the male inhabitants shall be
married men. The larger proportion, probably, would
be single men or men whose wives remained in their
native village.

In the matter of wage and food, rations or cash in
lieu of rations, with proper safeguards against want
and improvidence, could be optional. That is to say,
should a native desire to provide for himself this
liberty might be given him with the stipulation that

[1] Such an innovation is already projected in England for town dwellers.

skoff for his needs be carried daily to the mine. Or,
alternatively, a daily or weekly ration be distributed,
the cost of additional rations for wife and family to be
deducted from his earnings. In large tribal kraals the
services of a chief or headman could be enlisted to
preside over the deliberations of his fellow-tribes-
men.

The effect of such a system would soon be felt in
Johannesburg. Slowly but surely a substantial class
of professional miner would take the place of the
present slippery individual. In many cases it would
induce a stay where otherwise an exodus takes place.
It does seem absurd after all the past years of mining
activity and vast amount expended in native wages that
recourse has to be had to the same primitive methods
of engaging labour as of yore. There has been no attempt to establish a permanent class of native miners.
In the days of liquor selling the native who expended
his earnings in drink became very often the best mining boy—for the reason that he had perforce to remain,
never saving the means to depart. Years of service,
broken as they were with weeks of carouse, soon made
the expert driller or machine boy. The method of
engagement and employment was and is still altogether
based upon a short service and rapid disappearance.
No efforts have been made to bind the ' boy ' closer
to his work or influence him to adopt mining work as
a profession. To-day effort is directed to obtain labour
further and further afield—British Central Africa,
Uganda, or China—while the natives nearer at hand are
abandoned without an effort to their present idle ways.
The mines already have their 60,000 to 70,000 boys
scattered along the Rand ; there seems nothing insuper-

able in containing them in specified native townships under control, instead of incarcerating them in numberless small and stuffy compounds. The day shifts and the night shifts can just as well be carried by rail or tram to their work as collected from the compound, and the change of surroundings will prove a relief from the everlasting pit before their eyes. Those who may elect to dwell at the mine may do so; those who prefer a proper location with kindred surroundings may enjoy this modest desire. The plan here outlined may prove worthy of considerable extension. Not only may churches and schools be provided, but also on Sundays and holidays so much innocent amusement as may delight the simple inhabitant. Occasional sport, physical and perhaps military training, technical instruction and other facilities, not enforced on the worker, but purely voluntary in attendance; and all who know the native, his curiosity and ambition to follow and ape the white man, will feel confident that the attendance will be there. Doubtless if some such policy had been adopted early in the Rand the native labour difficulty would have not grown to such proportions as it has. Ere this some thousands of miners would have been dwelling around the gold fields, and the young would have been apprenticed to the work from youth upwards. The same principle applies in other South African mines and industries. Instead of the perpetual round of engagement and desertion characteristic of native employment, a working population would have sprung up forming the connecting link between the select coloured artisan class and the raw native masses—a conduit or channel of industrial evolution solving the native labour problem. The essence of the plan is to substitute for the past and existing method of native housing a system of proper native habitations with domestic surroundings, established at or in the vicinity of the works, providing inducements for the labourers to make the location their home. The effect of such settlements, instead of the ordinary ' coloured ' locations of the towns—open to all coloured men, workers and loafers, wives and brothels alike—would be to stimulate civilisation and commerce, and attract many of the idle thousands from the crowded native settlements.

Enough has been said to indicate the proper lines to follow. There is nothing impracticable or unreasonable in the design. Perhaps Government assistance might be necessary—Government co-operation would be essential. As previously shown, it is vain to ignore the native in the future of South Africa. He shows no tendency to diminish or retreat before the advance of the whites. He must either work out his own salvation or salvation must be provided for him. If South Africans intend to do their duty, and shoulder ' the white man's burden,' then active measures should be taken for their own as for the native's sake to direct the native trend in the direction it should go.

CHAPTER XI

SOURCES OF LABOUR

LABOUR for the mines is drawn, or, to be more exact, originates, from various centres of native occupation. The main divisions commonly represented in actual mining work are, taking them in their degrees of importance, the East Coast and Zambesi, the Northern Transvaal, Basutoland, Cape Colony, Natal, Bechuanaland, and a small quantity from Zululand and Swaziland. Of these the East Coast or 'Portuguese' native takes prior rank in importance. From the densely populated 'Biyin' province of the late kingdom of Gungunhana large supplies have been drawn, both by voluntary emigration and by direct recruitment. The Tonga countries, on the Portuguese littoral, have provided another fruitful source ; while the natives dwelling on the banks of the Zambesi and adjacently have helped to swell the main stream of labour grouped under the denomination 'East Coast.' On the Rand these boys are known generically as Shangaans and Zambesis, whilst finer distinctions have termed them Tongas, Shangaans, M'Chopies, and Maputas, the latter a tribe dwelling on the East Coast between Zululand and the Tembe at Delagoa. The greater majority of these tribes speak the Tonga dialect, and a large proportion Zulu. They differ, however, from the purer Zulu type of Zululand, Swaziland, and Matabeleland by their greater industry, poorer physique, better tractability, and quicker habits of adaptability. These are the mainstay of the ' underground ' workings, taking much more readily to mining work proper than the Cape Colony or Transvaal native. The population of these districts is officially estimated at 1,500,000 souls, from which, according to the official statistics of the Chamber of Mines, some 39,000 are employed at work on the mines. The number recruited shows a proportion of about 2 per cent. of the estimated total population. Yet around Delagoa Bay, the centre, so to speak, of this East Coast native supply, the labour question is rearing its head. Since the Transvaal mines raised their wages, the boys who work about the railway and shipping are demanding 2s. 6d. to 3s. per day, and youngsters who formerly earned their 15s. to 30s. a month claim their 3l. The authorities, it is stated, have in mind the promulgation of a law, at an early date, which will fix a scale of pay and thus relieve the present friction. This autocratic measure is practicable under Portuguese government, but scarcely under the benign rule of the Britisher.

From the Transvaal proper, with its estimated population of 750,000, some 12,500 are shown as at work, which accounts for somewhat less than 2 per cent. of the total. From Basutoland and the Cape Colony, with their population of 262,561 and 1,059,141 respectively, some 6,000 are drawn, while Bechuanaland with its 122,000 estimated natives contributes 2,000, also showing about 2 per cent. of the whole. As the Transvaal and the Bechuanaland natives are the tribes nearest the Rand, while the East Coast boys,

though distant, take most readily to mining labour, it
almost appears that under existing circumstances 2 to
3 per cent. of the total population is the proportion
which has recourse to the mines for work. As the
native population south of the Zambesi is estimated
at something like 5,000,000, if the same proportion
could be generally applied this would make a possible
total for mining purposes of 100,000 boys. But from this
purely speculative estimate the 1,000,000 boys from the
Cape Colony, whose work lies nearer home, contribut-
ing but a very small fraction of the total, must be
excepted; therefore if 80,000 were adopted as an
hypothetical mean, the figure would be nearer the
mark. Yet, as is shown, some 100,000 boys were
actually employed before the war, so that it is evident
this number may again be expected to materialise at
some future date—early or deferred.

It is, however, self-evident that any estimate as to
native labour available for work in the mines of the
Transvaal must omit both the Cape Colony and Natal
from possible regions of supply. As shown by the
official returns, neither the Cape Colony nor Natal
provides any material assistance, and this is explained
by the figures furnished to the Natal Legislative
Assembly by the Secretary for Native Affairs. He
claims that the native population of Natal totals
800,000, and of these estimates that some 200,000 are
adult males capable of work. He also affirms that the
great majority of these had at some time or other been in
the employment of white men. Now Natal in addition
to its great native population employed about 70,000
Indian coolies, and at work which should be congenial
to the Kafir, certainly neither above nor beneath his

capacity. The Cape is similarly constituted, for the relatively large European population of the Cape Colony (say 500,000), with its large towns, busy seaports, its diamond mines, its coal mines, and a great agricultural industry, have need of all the coloured labour within its boundaries. Basutoland can also be little depended upon ; for a large portion of the natives of this picturesque country are producers themselves, growing great quantities of grain and farming cattle, horses, and sheep. It is from this native territory that the Orange River Colony draws the greater portion of its labouring population.

As evidence of the hopelessness of this territory as an effective labour source, the communication from Messrs. Fraser, of Wepener, the agents for the Rand Chamber of Mines, speaks almost decisively. As read at a meeting of that Chamber in June of this year (1903) it was to the effect as follows :

' Lerothodi and chiefs discourage boys going for six
' months. For this reason and better labour offering
' nearer home we anticipate scant success. We suggest
' your altering terms to four months immediately. I
' learn from chiefs that from Lerothodi downwards they
' are all opposed to a six months' contract, that Basutos
' have to plough, sow, and reap, and have families, which
' the Portuguese boys evidently have not, and cannot go
' away for so long. I will remind you that this has been
' the objection raised by Lerothodi from the very com-
' mencement, and in regard to the letter you sent me he
' says that he cannot urge his boys to go to the mines for
' so long as six months. Owing to this fact and the
' increased activity of all recruiting agents concerned,
' who have raised their wages and reduced their term of

'employment to from one to three months, as I told you,
'I may not have given it a fair trial, and shall renew my
'exertions this month, but the result will be we shall not
'recruit more than 100 boys or perhaps 150 this month.
'The men I have in employ are very much discouraged,
'as they say they cannot compete with other agents, and
'that it is absurd to suppose that any boys will come on
'a six months' contract for 60s. when they can get the
'same price at Bloemfontein or on the railways for one,
'two, or three months' engagement. . . . Boiled down,
'the whole fact of the failure is this—that there are
'three employers for every boy that wants to work.'

The Bechuanaland protectorate, which borders the
Transvaal to the west, is not a very thickly populated
country, and the natives cannot boast of the physique
nor the industry required of the efficient mining boy. As
a recruiting ground for labour it is not in favour, although
it does provide a quota to the sum total of labour.
Rhodesia is equally out of the reckoning. Some 6,000
to 7,000 natives are employed at the mines, of which
only about 1,000 may be said to belong locally. This
northern centre also mainly depends upon the East
Coast native for labour, more than a half of the total
coming from outside, mainly from the Shangaan
country. Yet to the west and north-west of Farther
Rhodesia lie two centres of native occupation—N'Gami-
land and Barotseland; north and north-east again are the
Zambesi tribes, the Angoni and the Batoka. Though
there are no means of ascertaining the real number of
the population in these distant centres, yet there is
sufficient evidence that, granting it as material, the
mass of these sable aborigines have not yet been in-
fected with any burning desire to offer themselves for

work. But really these 'teeming millions' of interior natives dwindle in numbers as one approaches them in examination. It is estimated that in Matabeleland, on March 31, 1903, the total native population was 187,182, of whom 32,157 are reckoned to be able-bodied men. On that date, according to Mr. Taylor, the chief native commissioner, there were employed in Matabeleland approximately 10,000 on general mining purposes, 9,000 on other than mining work, and 4,000 on railway construction and maintenance. Colonel Heyman, quoting Mr. Taylor at a Chamber of Mines meeting, said : ' It would appear at first sight that 23,000 out of ' the 32,000 were employed in one way or another apart ' from agriculture. But Mr. Taylor adds that of the ' total number of natives employed on the mines, not ' more than 20 per cent. are drawn from local Matabele- ' land and Mashonaland sources, and that the majority of ' these are employed in surface works and wood-cutting. ' The average number of natives from Portuguese ' territory is 55 per cent. of the total number employed ' in the mines ; they include Shangaans, Nyambans, and ' Abachopi. Fifteen per cent. are drawn from north of ' the Zambesi, and 10 per cent. from the other territories. ' Of the 32,157 able-bodied men in Matabeleland, only ' 15,641 have worked for three months during the ' year. The above figures refer only to Matabeleland, ' but I have been furnished with other figures referring ' to the whole of Southern Rhodesia. The requirements ' of Southern Rhodesia on March 31 were placed at ' 16,335 for the mines and 19,500 for other employments, ' making in all 35,835. We were short, however, of ' 4,930 for the mines and of 2,500 for other employments, ' leaving a shortage of 7,430, and thus making the actual

' number at work 28,405. Of this number 13,846 came
' from outside our boundaries, so showing only 14,559
' as the number of local natives at work at any one
' time.'

It is consequently seen that as far as Rhodesia is
concerned the Rand has little to expect from that
quarter. In fact, according to Colonel Heyman, within
the next two years Rhodesia will require an additional
21,000 natives for the mines alone, or 66,800 in all,
without reckoning other employments. As analysed
by the same gentleman, 'If we make a generous allow-
' ance, and assume that each native will work only four
' months during the year, it would require slightly over
' 200,000 able-bodied male adults to provide for our
' requirements. The estimated total native population
' is 510,000, of whom there would be available for
' work, as able-bodied male adults, 110,000, or about
' one-half our requirements. Of the 28,000 at present at
' work, some 13,800 come from beyond our boundaries,
' thus showing that 14,200 or slightly more than half
' are natives of Southern Rhodesia, or about 12 per cent.
' of the adult male population.

'There is, of course,' continues Colonel Heyman,
' Northern Rhodesia to fall back upon, with its esti-
' mated population of 600,000, of whom 140,000 are said
' to be able-bodied male adults. A considerable allow-
' ance must be made for the requirements of Northern
' Rhodesia itself, where the development of the copper
' mines will be undertaken this year on a large scale,
' and but a very small allowance reduces the number
' below the 200,000 in Southern and Northern Rhodesia
' that are necessary to meet our requirements in the
' almost immediate future.'

In addition to this gloomy outlook for mining labour, it is asserted that not alone labour is wanted for the mines in Rhodesia, but also for households, farming, railway construction, and other industries. Wages of natives as domestic servants have gone up at least 50 per cent., and the same rise has taken place in regard to farm labourers.

Summing up, as far as British South Africa is concerned, the hope of materially increasing the present supply of native labour is very slender. Sir Richard Solomon, speaking in the Transvaal Legislative Council, in reply to a query from Sir Percy Fitzpatrick, stated : ' It was generally agreed that the number of natives, ' men, women, and children, south of the Zambesi, did ' not exceed six millions. But there was considerable ' difference of opinion as to the number of males capable ' of work, and as to the proportion of those who could ' be counted on as likely to leave their districts for work ' on the mines and other large industries. No estimate, ' however, was put forward which indicated the possibility ' of any considerable addition to the number of natives ' at present employed outside their own districts. The ' members of the Bloemfontein Conference most inti- ' mately acquainted with the districts containing the ' largest native population were all unable to hold out ' any hope of a great increase in the supply of labour ' from the regions with which they were severally ' familiar.'

Undoubtedly it is the Portuguese territories on the East Coast which yield the greater portion of Transvaal supply as far as South Africa is concerned. The Delagoa Bay correspondent of a Rand paper ascertained from the various Governors of the different districts the latest statistics of the number of able-bodied men in the following East Coast areas :

Lourenço Marques	.	.	110,000
Inhambane .	.	.	140,000
Gazaland	.	.	60,000
Mozambique .	.	.	80,000
Zambesia	.	.	90,000
Total	.	.	480,000

It was asserted that in addition to this number many thousands may be found in the interior of Mozambique and around Nyassa. But of course, even if the estimate be accurate, only a proportion may be induced to leave their homes for work, and of this again a percentage only would go to the mines; though the East Coast has the advantage of other sources in that the conditions locally and in the surroundings are not such as reign in British South Africa, with its heavy draught on the labour supply created by mining and commercial demands other than gold mining.

In Central Africa the nearest important centre of native occupation is Nyassaland, and steps have already been taken to procure supplies from those parts. British Nyassaland, which is almost identical in geographical expression with British Central Africa, lies between the southernmost point of Lake Tanganyika and follows the western littoral of the lake from which the district takes its name. Numerous tribes of Bantu derivation inhabit these regions, such as Angoni, Atongas, Yaos, and Makololo. None of these races appear to be promising material, according to travellers visiting them. No estimate of the actual population of these regions appears to have been hazarded, but it can scarcely be a considerable one, either in the aggregate or per square mile. Though steps are now in progress to tap these sources, and a thousand or two may be obtained and perhaps annually recruited, there is nothing to warrant any hope of solving the labour problem by a recourse to this locality. Portuguese Nyassaland, lying between the lake Nyassa and the sea, though fairly largely populated, is under foreign domination, and carefully farmed by the English Company trading under charter of the Portuguese Government. The natives appear fairly industrious in their occupations, and besides subsist largely on the banana, a food foreign to Transvaal cultivation. The nearest great source of native supply in Central Africa is undoubtedly Uganda. Sir Harry Johnston first drew attention to the possibility of this territory as a recruiting ground for Rand labour. But the recommendation brought a hornets' nest about his ears ; the missionary societies loudly and emphatically protesting against any exodus of the population from this centre of their activity. The Bishop of Uganda sent a long letter to the *Times* on the subject, wherein, while appreciating Sir Harry Johnston's good intentions, he contends that ' even Sir Harry Johnston is unable to ' alter the physical conditions of Central and Southern ' Africa. In spite of him Uganda must still remain in ' the tropics and under the equator, whilst South Africa ' must continue in its sub-tropical place, subject to all ' those climatic changes which, while they are endurable ' and even pleasurable to those brought up in a tem- ' perate climate, are deadly in the extreme to such ' people as the Baganda, accustomed as they are to ' the perpetual summer of their earthly paradise.   How

' extremely subject to diseases of the lungs and respiratory
' organs the Baganda are, and how ill adapted to the
' endurance of climatic changes, has been proved over
' and over again by sad experience. . . . A large num-
' ber of porters was needed to take the Indian contingent
' of some 500 men to rail-head. Basoga and Baganda
' were employed in the work. It is almost incredible,
' but it is nevertheless a fact, that more than 2,000 lives
' were sacrificed in the operation. Dysentery was
' largely responsible, I believe, for this great loss. . . .
' The fact is that people like the Baganda and Basoga,
' who live almost entirely on the plantain, are unable to
' adapt themselves to a grain diet without grave danger
' to life. . . . It is my firm conviction, and also the
' opinion of every missionary, Anglican or Roman, with
' whom I have discussed the question,' says the Bishop,
' that if allowed to go to South Africa for labour in the
' mines the natives of Uganda will simply die like flies.
' But let us suppose that we are mistaken, and that it is
' possible for the Baganda to live and labour in South
' Africa. What follows? An annual withdrawal from
' Uganda of thousands of its most vigorous labourers.
' . . . Already it has been and is being drawn upon
' to an alarming extent. . . . I cannot close without
' one brief yet earnest appeal on behalf of that work
' which, baptized in the blood of martyrs, has been
' further consecrated by the noble self-sacrifice and
' devotion of those who, counting not their lives
' dear unto themselves, have laid them down (two
' within the last fortnight) in the prosecution of
' their missionary labours in these regions. I do not say
' that this work, so blessed and consecrated, is in danger
' of destruction by the proposed opening of Uganda to

' labour enlistment. It rests, I am convinced, on too
' sure a basis for that. But that it will be marred and
' hindered, if not actually imperilled, seems certain.'
The right reverend gentleman, in this protest,
places what appears to us the main reason of his
objection last. Though it is quite conceivable that
the Baganda native might not at first thrive in the
different conditions reigning in the Rand, yet in view
of the fact that other tribes from tropical climes live
quite comfortably there, and that the climate is not
unkindly in the Transvaal, the fear that the Baganda
would die on the Rand is scarcely convincing. In
view of the natives' disinclination to leave their own
country and the opposition of the trader and the
missionary, Uganda is now ruled out of consideration.

As a matter of fact the further one goes afield from
South Africa—south of the Zambesi—for raw native
labour, the greater the obstacles and the objection to
imported black labour. Somalis have been tried and
found wanting. On the West Coast labour is not too
plentiful, and the natives in the Congo and Gold Coast
regions are so dissimilar to those on the East in
custom and race that one might just as well import
Arabs, Asiatics, or Kanakas. Furthermore the greater
commerce in native products of West Africa leaves
little labour to spare, even for the gold mining of those
regions. When such distant sources are contemplated
one might well ask if the game is worth the candle.
To transport raw and untrained natives thousands
of miles to take up occupations in settled industrial
mining regions smacks of absurdity except under
undisguised slavery, which no one wants.

CHAPTER XII

THE NATIVE AS A WORKER AND CUSTOMER

UPON contact with Europeans, Kafirs take to work readily, if not effectively, accept their position unreservedly, and soon become aware of the value of money. In fact, they acknowledge the ' white man ' as *baas* and strive to imitate him. The Kafir whom an up-country resident comes into contact with mostly in every-day life is the ' kitchen boy.' Two ladies rarely meet together ' in chat ' without in some manner or other Tom or Jim, the kitchen boy, cropping up in conversation. One bemoans his departure to *hamba kia* (go home), and feels lost without him; the other, on the other hand, declares that *hers* is the bane of her life, and worries her to death with his awkward and stupid ways. One quotes his cleverness, the other his stupidity. A lady straight from home and not in the position to support a staff of white servants soon finds that ' the kitchen boy ' is a problem to be solved before she can have peace or comfort. If she is careless and easy he robs her, if sharp and shrewish he leaves her; if she is quick and energetic he lets *her* do all the work, and if slow and apathetic he does it his own way and in his own time. A good kitchen boy is an article which, once possessed, should be kept as long as possible, as the species is not plentiful. In

engaging a kitchen boy there are two or three golden
rules that can be followed with much advantage.
Never take a boy that talks a lot, and who declares
himself a kind of 'Admirable Crichton,' as he is
generally too knowing. A kraal boy is mostly
preferable to a missionary boy (unless the latter be
specially recommended), as the professing Christian has
a tendency to go out at awkward times under the cloak
of religion, ostensibly to attend school or church, but
actually for a stroll with a few lady friends. A kraal
boy rarely has such friends—he is too virtuous.
Endeavour to engage a boy whom you can understand
and who will understand you. Always give a boy full
current wages, but promise no extras, as once you tip
him for any extra work he will always expect it, and
if you once fail to give it him a grievance is established.
Never be too familiar or laugh and joke with a native
servant, as familiarity breeds contempt. As most
'boys' understand a little English, one must be careful
and not praise him while he is present, or pity him in
any shape, such as when he has carried a heavy load
or worked long hours, as Kafirs do not appreciate pity,
and next time you wish him to do a similar thing he
will at once complain and grumble. If you *wish* to
reward him for extra work, do not promise him beforehand or even give instantly on completion, but a little
time afterwards, when you will discover that it is
better appreciated, as he has not expected it. Always
perform your promise to him, whether it be a reward
or a thrashing; he respects you for it. If you possess
a good Kafir you must wink a great deal at his petty
faults, as even black humanity is not faultless; should
he err venially try to put him in the right path, but if

he wilfully disobeys it must be rectified with a firm hand, even at risk of parting. Kafirs are trained to do all the work of an English cook, scullerymaid, waiter, butler, valet, or major-domo. The native is also largely employed as a nurse to male children, and in some cases to children of either sex. So much confidence has been reposed in the Kafir servant that mistresses have come to regard him more as a machine than a human being. On the whole, this confidence has not been abused, although now and then cases occur which serve as a lurid warning against the practice of employing natives in too close domestic service. Sometimes the ignorance of the native, added to the imperfect knowledge of the language by the mistress, leads to disastrous errors. For instance, a case is reported at Johannesburg where a mistress told her ' boy ' to boil an egg and time the boiling by the clock. The mistress waited for her egg to be served, but the boy not appearing she repaired to the kitchen to chide him, when, lo and behold ! the saucepan was merrily boiling on the fire with the clock inside, and the boy was waiting for the egg to cook on the table, wondering at the white people's magic !

Another story is related of a lady leaving her kitchen boy to cook the dinner. Among other things a pie was to be baked. On her return from visiting, the dinner was served, but the pie looked a little sickly and off-coloured. The lady interrogated the boy as to the cause. After a deal of prevarication he stated that the pie had got burnt and turned black; he therefore had carefully scraped it and washed it with soap and water to make it appear presentable. A Kafir boy was once ordered to kill a fowl for dinner. A quarter of an hour afterwards the master had occasion to go out in the yard, where a curious sight met his view. The poor fowl was running about the yard *plucked*. The boy had reversed the usual process and had plucked the poor fowl before killing it.

Few people have taken the trouble to think what it means to a Kafir coming to Johannesburg, as has been his custom, to seek work. It must be to him in a humble and simple fashion what centuries ago it was to our ancestors in the age of the Crusades, a strange and eventful pilgrimage. The parallel may be a little far-fetched, and the object of the quest totally different, but on the other hand the results are very similar. People of all nations in Europe were bound to the one place, the road was comparatively unknown, the vicissitudes many, and return uncertain. Those returning were looked upon as great travellers, and brought with them many evidences of the higher civilisation which those at home had been strangers to. So it is with travelling natives, at least the bulk of them, those arriving from distant northern regions, for those from the south and east are better versed in European life. Imagine them at their homes leading a peaceful and pastoral life, unbroken with the exception of an occasional raid, each equally at home in his family circle, with parents, sweethearts, or wives and children, leaving them all for a long journey and a dubious return. A small party collect together; they consist of a few middle-aged married men, some young fellows, and perhaps three or four youngsters, all bound for ' I'Gold ' or ' Joshberg,' as they term it, to obtain the wherewithal to buy wives, cattle, and luxuries. They are con-

ducted a distance along the footpath by the whole
kraal population, their women carrying their loads,
until the spot is reached where adieux have to be said,
and they step out for good with a long glance back to
those whom perhaps they may never see again. In a
few days they cross the borders of their own country,
and at once become strangers in the land they walk.
They cross other native territories, sleep at different
kraals on the road, become embroiled in a Kafir beer
fight ; one gets knocked on the head, and they have to
bury him. They travel further, arrive in the Transvaal, and, as occurred before the British *régime*, a Boer
persuades them to work on his farm for a month or
so. In a couple of days they find him a hard and
rough taskmaster, and they clear. The Boer rides
after them, collars them, and brings them before the
Field-cornet; they get twenty-five lashes each, one boy
sickens from the effect, they leave him at a passing
kraal and he promptly dies. They arrive at Johannesburg at last with ranks slightly thinned. Then they
settle down to work; one or two of them become
habitual drunkards, or at least did so before liquor was
taboo, forget the *intombi* they are working for, and
squander the money as it is earned. One gets killed in
the mine, and in six or twelve months, out of fifteen or
twenty starting, there only remain a dozen to return.
Then they have to undergo the same risks on returning,
but joining a larger gang they provide mutual protection.
They arrive home, are joyfully welcomed, for they are
now *men*. They sport shirts and trousers, there is a
blanket for the mother, beads for the girls and sweethearts, and a nice long overcoat for the ' old boss.'
They run about arrayed in bright handkerchiefs, and

one shows a curious glass that magnifies, whilst the other discourses sweet (?) music from a ' costina,' and so all is gay. So much for the journey.

Of course the description may be modified to-day, when better order is preserved in the outside districts and the irresponsible powers of the Boer Veld-cornet are terrors of the past.

Kafirs working at the mines are of a good many nationalities. They do not intermingle, but each tribe keeps strictly together. Two of the same kind rarely quarrel, as they can always find accommodation with men of other tribes, with the advantage of prompt assistance from their own. Talking is the bulk of matter in a fight. Two boys of different nationalities have a row; they at once proceed to murder each other—with the mouths; their friends join in, they get warm to it, and weapons are sought for. If these same weapons were effectually used half the combatants would be killed at the first brush, for they consist of long $\frac{3}{4}$-inch iron bolts, pieces of iron piping, knobkerries studded with brass nails, not omitting to mention stones as large as cannon balls. In a Kafir row these things are flourishing around, and an inexperienced onlooker would shut his eyes in horror. But when he opens them again—the actors are still shouting. At length one party becomes more numerous than the other; the smaller body starts a judicious retreat, which ends in flight. One of the pursuers, braver than the rest, rushes forward and manages to give probably the quietest of the other tribe a wipe over the head with a piston rod, or something like it; the man drops, he gets another wipe over the other side and he stiffens. With a triumphant yell the brave man beats a retreat to his fellows. White assistance reaches the spot, the combatants are dispersed and retire to their respective quarters ; but the noise is now redoubled. Just before one gang was shouting, but now there are two, each discussing the affair, and continuing until midnight. Meanwhile the unfortunate victim has been carried away on a stretcher to the hospital, where they find a side of his skull caved in. The doctor plasters it up, and the boy is seen the following day with a towel round his head 'chewing the rag' over a threepenny handkerchief in the nearest store to the compound. Boys, however, happily do other things than fight— they work. Some are more industrious than others. Some become quite skilled in their work, wield the drilling hammer with precision if not with vigour, and fire holes like Cornishmen—sometimes. They become at once ' S'good boy,' as they express it, tie up their trousers at the knees, navvy fashion, and adopt a patronising air with the *mambarers*, or raw 'uns.

In the days, now happily departed, when drink of the vilest description and in abundance was obtainable, there existed a type called the *Isidakewa*, or drunkard. In a store where the boys' belongings were hanging, a drunkard's sack was generally noticeable by its age, and leanness of aspect. With his first month's wages he bought a few articles for cash, more on credit, then reckoned he was a rich man, and got drunk on the balance. During the following month he borrowed money from his friends to satisfy his craving, resulting at the end of the month, on pay-day, in his having a few interested pals waiting for him. He then repaid 50 per cent. of his loan, stood liquors with the balance, and became indignant when refused further 'tick' at

the store. His shirt rotted on his back, for he could
not spare money enough to buy another. The time
arrived when his former companions tied up their sacks
in preparation for their return home, with purses
lined with gold : he was penniless and meandering
about in a sottish state, and they left without him.
Sometimes, after a year or two, he would see the error
of his ways, drop the liquor, pull himself together, and
return home at last ; but in most instances he drank
year in and year out, until he was either knocked on
the head in a drunken brawl, fell down a shaft on a
dark night, or something equally happy occurred and
put him out of his misery.

Native life in a compound is singularly free from
care. The Kafir has his regular meals provided for
him, meat at intervals, and his movements are free
when off duty. Serious crimes amongst them are rare,
as the law courts can show. The native criminal-
sheet is mostly recruited from the town Kafirs and
general black loafers. When a mine boy is not
working, he is either at the store inspecting his goods
and chattels, asleep, or lying outside threading beads
or wiring knobkerries. He buys bread largely, which
he eats with sugar water, and goes in for such other
luxuries as cooked meat, condensed milk (used as
jam), and golden syrup. When pay-day arrives there
is much sorting up, debts are settled all round (they
largely borrow of one another), and those so inclined
have a good carouse of beer.

In companies where there is one pay-day in the
month work is sometimes at a standstill for the first
couple of days after, but a much better plan is to pay
the boys independently, as their monthly wages become

due, so that they are not all paid at the same time. Just previous to pay-day many are the inquiries to the storekeeper as to the amount of wages on the work ticket, of which they seem to be ever in doubt. On receipt of their wages they hasten to their respective quarters in the compound, where small groups are formed by the different mates, and distribute the money to one or another according to their respective rights. Youngsters are giving their money to their elder brothers or guardians, some are paying off their debts, and others are stowing their money away. You will probably observe a small group where one Kafir takes all the money from his comrades. It is a syndicate— a disease very prevalent in Johannesburg. Every month, by rotation, one of the members receives his mates' money for sole benefit, so that it is either a feast or a famine with them. Where the excitement of the investment comes in is the hope deferred for a few months ; when the turn comes to receive, the lucky one gets a lump sum which makes him a rich man suddenly —always provided the previously lucky ones have not left before his turn comes, in which case he has to start and collect for himself. At last all affairs are settled, and they are busy stacking away the coin in the farthest corner of their money-belts ; some stroll off to the store and buy that particular article that they have been longing for, and others adjourn to the eating-house, where they sit on a plank before a dish of roughly-cooked meat with plenty of gravy (?), price 6d. In the days when liquor was obtainable some trooped to the canteen, perhaps a group of about eight or nine boys, who invested in, say, four bottles of liquor at 2s. 6d. per bottle. These they stuffed in their shirts or under their blankets, and walked into the veld to some unfrequented spot, where they squatted and drank, and had a nice comfortable carouse. The procedure was generally as follows: Opening the first bottle, they served out its contents and started some weighty argument *re* the manners and customs of Europeans. Tapping the second bottle, they became merrier; much laughter is aroused by a clever imitation of the compound manager's broken kitchen Kafir as he drives them to their work. One boy relates with great glee how he had managed to steal a pair of boots from the store by sliding them under his blanket, and they all relate funny stories. At the third bottle the conversation has veered round, by some means, to an old quarrel that had occurred several months ago at their kraal, and accord becomes discord. All are shouting at once, angry passions rise; they are just coming to blows when one of the party, with a drunken lurch, falls helpless to the ground. The argument is forgotten, and they all try, with much jabbering, to put their comrade on his feet, but without avail; so they elect to carry him home. He objects, strikes out with hands and feet, but numbers prevail, and, at the sacrifice of his three shirts, which are torn to shreds from his back in layers, they lift him up, and a mass of struggling arms and legs is seen to be meandering across the veld with many and ludicrous undulations, just, for all the world, like a gigantic centipede.

But a Kafir is not only a producer at the goldfields; he is also a large consumer. The Kafir trade is an important source of revenue to the Government and profit to the mercantile community. It is surprising to one not acquainted with the Kafir trade how wide is the range of their purchases, after observing them at work in the mine, attired with a towel around their body, and nought else. They purchase such opposite articles as condensed milk and pain-killer for consumption ; three-guinea suits of clothes and a threepenny handkerchief for apparel ; a cotton sheet at 1s. 6d. and a woollen rug at 25s. ; a shilling cotton shirt and a seven-and-sixpenny woollen one. When a boy is dressed at his best he generally shows his nationality. A Basuto will wear a tweed suit, linen shirt, hard felt hat, and stylish boots ; a Zulu affects a serviceable pair of old soldier's pants and a policeman's overcoat ; a Shangaan scorns trousers, but sports two undervests, three shirts and two waistcoats, worn accumulatively, with a gradation of dirt which gets thicker as they approach the skin—for the new goes over the old until the sub-stratum drops away from senile decay—the wearer or the garment. An Imhambane native's favourite attire is a soft felt hat, digger's boots and an overcoat doing the rest of the duty; an M'Chopie delights in rags of any texture or shape.

Kafirs are strange customers to deal with, for they have their own humorous way of purchasing. Patience is the great quality required in a Kafir store. Their mode of dealing differs but slightly, but for sheer cussedness the Shangaan takes the cake. He wishes to purchase a shirt, so at once gathers as many of his brothers together as he can conveniently lay hold of as advisers, and they accompany him to the store to see fair play. They enter the store ; the salesman is behind the counter waiting for customers. They approach the shop counter and run their eyes along the shelves, looking at everything *except the coveted shirt.* One *who does not wish to purchase anything* approaches a 25s. overcoat hanging from the ceiling and nonchalantly asks the price. The perhaps unsophisticated assistant at once plucks up heart at the hope of a good sale, and answers blandly, 25s. At hearing the price all the company look up with intense astonishment and disgust, suggesting that he is joking, for, as they protest, in the other store the same article is sold for 10s. The salesman inwardly rages at their mendacity, but suppresses his feelings. He says carelessly that it must be another kind with not quite so much *wool* (?) in it. (This is a kind of by-play with them to mystify you as to their real requirement.) They all leave the overcoat, and one of them discovers a good pair of riding breeches hanging in front of the counter, and asks the price. You know they don't wear trousers, so you tell them 5s.; they think it very cheap, but tell you to put it back. Your patience then gets exhausted, and you ask them with emphasis, ' What the devil do you want?' At length the real purchaser says a shirt. 'Price?' 'Eighteenpence.' You show them an eighteenpenny shirt; they measure it, look at its texture, examine the seams, return it to your hands as worthless, and demand a better one. And so it continues until they get suited.

But your troubles have only just started, for the money has to be obtained, and this was a popular method of paying: The treasurer of the party stood firmly on his extended feet in the middle of the store; his friends formed a circle round him, one seized his arm, extended it, and started tucking up the sleeves of the various shirts on his body. At length a leather

band came to view; this they unstrap; it is hollow,
with a small slit three parts down as an aperture.
Then the pantomime commenced ; for the money is
firmly imbedded furthest away from the opening.
They squeeze the thong ; they slap it on the counter ;
they strive to press the money out with their fingers ;
they hold it on high, blowing air into it, until either
the money falls into their mouths and nearly chokes
them, or in desperation you take a knife, cut the blessed
belt open, and present them with a new one. At length
you are paid, but your troubles are still not over, for
a haggle for a *bonsella* (present) now ensues, which you
eventually terminate by giving them a box of matches
or a halfpenny snuff box, and the bargain is then
concluded. A Zulu or Colony Kafir deals in a different
style, though equally exasperating. He walks into
the store with the air of a millionaire, pushes all your
other customers aside, and demands 3*d*. tobacco, then
3*d*. sugar, then 3*d*. matches. He examines critically
the quality and quantity of each article, essays a
grumble, and retires like a lord.

The best native to deal with is undoubtedly the
Transvaal Basuto, who buys what he wants, does not
haggle, and calls for the best—price no object.

Their ideas of quality in the different articles are
curious. Boots must squeak as they walk ; clothing
must be soft, tight fitting, with pockets galore ; blankets
must be opaque and large ; bread must not be baked
brown, and ginger beer must pop.

The different tribes affect different articles in buying.
Inhambanes smoke cigars, but reverse the European
fashion by placing the lighted end in the mouth and
the pointed end outwards. This works well when

calm and collected, but if an argument ensues and one
of them gets the cigar rammed down his throat it
becomes embarrassing, not to say painful. Offer a
cigar to a Shangaan and you offend him : he asks you
in scorn if you take him for an Inhambane. Basutos
buy rugs with circular patterns on them, Shangaans
prefer squares or striped patterns. Some natives are
very vain and nothing delights them more than to
stand before a large mirror and admire themselves. If
you be watchful you will observe them admire their
teeth, count the pimples on their faces, pull out stray
wool, and caress their scanty beards. They will also
examine the whites of their eyes, sing and gesticulate
to themselves, and pose with infinite gusto, fancying
themselves great swells. In a store where there is a
nice mirror they will often, upon passing, enter one
door, stand and admire themselves for a few minutes,
exit by the further door, and continue on their errand.
It is good sport watching them with a photo of some
one they know well. You place the likeness in their
hands and ask them if they know whom it represents.
They hold it by one corner obliquely before them,
gaze stupidly at it, examine the edges carefully, look
blankly at the back of it, and can make neither head
nor tail of it. You then snatch it from their hands,
and place it flat upon the counter before them. You
point out the eyes —a smile of recognition illumines
their faces ; they say to each other ' By Jove,' or
rather the Kafir equivalent, *Mybábé*, ' these *are* eyes ' ;
then you show them the nose and other features by
rotation. As you proceed with your explanation a
broad grin is wafted across their countenances, until
a chorus of voices is heard laughing and shouting

out the name of the original. The recognition is then complete.

Kafirs occasionally have rare fun at the expense of the harassed storekeeper: One of their delights is to march into the store, and with great demeanour ask to be shown a concertina. One is proffered them and a member of the gang tries it. With hands down and bowed head he will din into your ears a hideous discord, all repetitions and no variations; then they examine the keys, ask the price, say it is too dear and demand another. You give them another; meanwhile another individual has seized upon the first one and tries its tune with the serious air of a connoisseur, whilst the second one is being operated upon by the first party. They play merrily together for about five minutes, the other mates strike up a jig with their feet, and they all thoroughly enjoy themselves—while the storekeeper is grinding his teeth. At last the exasperated salesman demands angrily if they intend buying. Should they respect his prowess they then cease, place the instruments on the counter, and innocently acquaint him with the fact that they have no money at present, but intend returning at the end of the month; but if, on the contrary, he has a name for meekness, they will not deign to answer but will walk out with a great air of offence.

Another amusement to the evil-minded native busybody is to walk into the store when many customers are buying. He joins the first group, criticises the goods, says the trousers do not fit, the coat is too dear, and leaves them all dissatisfied, to stroll to the next lot. They are perhaps buying a blanket; he will take it from the purchaser's hands, measure it, find out a small hole, damage both the storekeeper's and the blanket's reputation, and with an innocent air stroll off to some other place of amusement. If the salesman kicks him out of the place he spoils what business is going on, and perhaps loses the run of some of the goods in the confusion, so he has to pocket the insult and wait patiently for an opportunity for reprisals.

As an artisan or workman, as set out in a previous chapter, the native has his limitations. But he is sturdy, brawny, and cheerful. He delights in working in smithies, in stables, in carpentering, and any vocations from whose height he can look contemptuously down upon his fellow. But the employment of raw natives in skilled handiwork often leads to farce and sometimes to tragedy—when the employer is short-tempered. It is narrated of an owner of a saw mill that he employed a native to attend the engine. One day the boiler required filling before firing, when he called the native to him and endeavoured to explain the working of the water gauge. He instructed him to fill the boiler and when the water in the gauge indicated a certain mark he should cease. The owner left on an errand and returned in an hour, when he found the boy standing ankle deep in water and covered with perspiration glowering at the water gauge. He had been pouring bucket after bucket of water *over the glass tube* in vain endeavours to achieve the desired result. History relates that the owner wiped the floor with the ' boy.' Poor chap, to this day the native could not see the harm he had done to deserve the chastisement.

But the Kafir is at his glory when acting as policeman. The native policeman may be seen in the height of his glory in Natal; but in other parts this particularly glorious luminary also shines. He is generally a Zulu, a masterful and sturdy type, but in some localities only masquerades under this tribal nomenclature, puffed up with pride of uniform, with hat rakishly cast on one side and knobkerrie in hand or in belt. The native policeman is a terror to his colour and a faithful and courteous servant to the European. He will greet a drunken brother with a kick from his bootless feet and objurgate him as a 'dirty black nigger.' Invariably true to his salt—the premature experiment in Matabeleland, where the police joined the insurgents, marks a rare exception—the duties of control under authority peculiarly appeal to the native imbued with love of order and obedience, irrespective of family or tribal ties. It has often been wondered why such splendid material is ignored by the Colonial and War Offices in aid of their 'little' wars.

PART III

WEST AND WEST-CENTRAL AFRICA

CHAPTER XIII

INHABITANTS

THE name of West Africa, it may be premised, in dealing with this subject, is used in its full local sense as embracing the country extending between the rivers Senegal and Congo, a distance of some 3,000 miles. The particulars given and conditions examined apply primarily, though not entirely, to British West Africa and to the Congo Free State. It has been deemed advisable to include the latter rather more fully than other foreign colonies in the scope of this brief review, as, in the first place, this State, lying mid-way between West Africa proper and South Africa, presents problems common to both and shows the latest experiments resulting from modern ideas of solution; and, in the second place, in order to examine conditions there in the light of common sense in view of the vast amount of nonsensical and exaggerated statements at present being served up to that section of the British public which appears to have an insatiable appetite, not to say *penchant*, for anything which it can construe into an 'African atrocity.'

In comparing the West African natives, their condition and status, with those of South Africa, we are faced with a far more complex and difficult problem than the one we have been hitherto dealing with. In South Africa the country at large may be said to be inhabited (with the exception of the so-called Malays and Cape Boys) by one great family of the human race —the Bantu negro—of a common origin and possessing certain well-marked characteristics. In West Africa this is far from being the case, the negro, though found throughout the country, existing in the interior over a large area only either in a hybrid form or as a subject of more powerful races of other origin. The question is further complicated by the fact that Mohammedanism and Fetichism exercise the vastest difference over the status and customs of the different territories or tribes in which they happen to be predominant. If is added to this the fact that foreign influence—European, Arab, and Berber—has for centuries been playing upon sections of the different peoples and modifying their opinions and forms of government, it will be seen that to attempt to generalise on the natives of West Africa as a whole would be utterly fallacious and in fact impossible. It will therefore be necessary to distinguish the true African race (the Negro and Bantu), the hybrid races of negro and North African union, and the races palpably of outside origin. The most that can be done, when descending into details, will be to select typical specimens of each class, it being clearly understood that what applies to one section does not necessarily apply to the other sections.

The true African race is held by some to be indigenous to the Soudan, where it is to-day known as the negro, and by others to the Central African forest, where it forms part of the Bantu peoples spread over Africa down to the Cape Colony. Be this as it may, at a very early period, perhaps the earliest in the history of man, the true negro race must have been found settled throughout the Soudan—that is to say, the immense stretch of fertile country extending from the Atlantic to the Nile and from the Sahara to the Great Forest—and with that portion of it known as the Western Soudan we are, in common with its coast regions, now immediately concerned.

This true negro population of the Western Soudan shows far more divergence in uniformity and style of life than does the Bantu branch of the human family, as throughout the interior it is found constantly crossed with fairer complexioned races (of Berber blood) and under the rule of warlike chiefs and castes of extraneous origin. The results of these changes, the Berber influence from the north, the Mohammedan conversion, the Arab emigration and conquests, and other causes, have, as already pointed out, naturally produced a great state of chaos from an ethnological standpoint, and, except in a few special regions, such as Southern Nigeria, it is very difficult to study the true negro in his pure form and original tribal state.

Roughly speaking, and as far as present knowledge goes, West Africa proper may be divided into : the negro coast natives, such as the Djolofs and Mandingoes of Senegal, the Susus of French Guinea, the Sofas in the Sierra Leone hinterland, the once powerful nations of Ashanti, Benin, and Dahomey, the Fantees of the Gold Coast, the Kroo, Mendis, Timinis, &c. of Sierra Leone and Liberia, and the natives of

Southern Nigeria (to mention only the most important) ; secondly, such nations as the Hausas (who are probably the result of a far-back intermixture of Berber blood with the true negro population of the interior country), the Yorubas, Nupés, and other people; and thirdly, races of acknowledged foreign origin, such as the Shuwa Arabs, Berber, Tuaregs, and (to enter on debateable ground) the well-known Fulani race. With regard to the latter, it is true Sir Harry Johnston is of opinion that these mysterious people are also of Berber or Berber and negro origin, but equally strong reasons (in which the writer shares) have been adduced to show that, like the ancient Songhay, the pure-bred Fulani can claim an eastern derivation. Reference may also be made to such nations as Borgu and Bornu, where direct evidence as to strong Berber immigration and settlement exists.

Turning now to the Bantu section of the negro race it is supposed, to quote Sir Harry Johnston again, that at a very early date, long before the Berber invasions of the Western Soudan, a Hamitic race, of mixed Caucasian and darker blood, emanating from a centre on the north-east coast, came in contact with the negro races of the great lakes, and so gave rise to the Bantu peoples who spread westward and southward until they peopled the whole of the great Central African forest, including what is now French and Portuguese Congo and the Congo Free State. In the former, however, the Fans, immortalised by Miss Kingsley, are generally considered as belonging to the negro and not to the Bantu type.

In the Congo Free State, the pure negro type is predominant in the north and north-east in the

fierce Mambatu, Niam-Niam, &c., and a hybrid
Negro-Bantu form in the Manyemas and Batetelas in
the east. Most of these Congolese negroes are noted
for their fierce and intractable dispositions (as well as
for propensities to cannibalism), and differ widely in
character from the somewhat more docile Bantu who
form the greater part of the population in the central,
southern, and western districts. An important branch
of this Bantu family exists also in the M'pongwe
(French Congo coast) and the Bangala (Upper
Congo). These two tribes form with others inland a
branch of the once powerful Bakongo group, the predominant people of the ancient 'kingdom of Congo,'
which was destroyed four centuries ago by the Portuguese. The population of the Congo Free State has
been variously estimated to-day at from 20,000,000 to
40,000,000 ; probably the truth lies about half way
between these two figures.

Of the other Congo Bantu tribes, the Balekas, occupying the shores of Stanley Pool, constitute a large
part of the native population west of Stanley Falls.
The Bayanzis are an important tribe of the Central
Congo, and in physique resemble the splendid Liberian
Kroo race—the sailors and boatmen of the West
African sea-coast. Their (the Bayanzis) principal
pursuits are fishing and boating, which they share
with the Bangalas as riverain workers. Mentally
they are considered the most intelligent of the inhabitants of the Congo Free State, and are very quick to
assimilate European ideas. The same remark also
applies to the Mombettus inhabiting the country
between the Arawumi and the Mbomu-Welle. The
Mongos, a well-known river tribe, are famous for their

strength and endurance, and form the bulk of the State's artillery forces.

The dwarf tribes are, owing to their mode of life, naturally not of much economic importance to the country, but they form an interesting problem for the student of ethnology. They are stated to be superior in intelligence to the blacks surrounding them, and though divided into four isolated tribes are believed to belong to the same race. The men average in height 4 ft., and are never known to exceed 4 ft. 6 in., but are physically well developed and exceedingly strong. The women are smaller in proportion but exceedingly prolific. They do not appear to live in regular villages but in temporary brushwood huts in the forest, and are of a nomadic disposition. Doubts have been expressed whether the Congo dwarfs are of African origin at all, but too little is known at present to express a definite opinion on this subject.

CHAPTER XIV

RELIGION

LEAVING on one side Christianity, which is referred to
in another chapter, the two great divisions of religion
in West Africa may be summed up in the words
Mohammedanism and Fetichism. The last is an awkward word, but it describes the state of the native mind
somewhat more accurately than the local European
one of paganism. Mohammedanism, be it said, is the
active proselytising religion of to-day, and fetichism
the stagnant crystallised beliefs which have for several
centuries been gradually disappearing before its attack.
To Mohammedanism, as such, no direct reference is
necessary, but in relation to its present and future
influence over its professors in West Africa some
attention must be given, as it seems destined at no
distant date to revolutionise the West African conditions as at present existing, and very possibly to evolve
a more or less homogeneous conglomeration of peoples
from a national point of view. About its effect in
raising the intellectual and moral standard of the
peoples who have adopted it there has never been any
question. Cannibalism, human sacrifices, and drunken-
ness are a few of the evils which its spread immediately
abolishes. Up to the present, Mohammedanism is
the only outside religious system which has ever exerted

wide-spread influence over the native mind, and it
appears to possess within itself qualities which exactly
fit it to the peculiar temperament of the negro and his
environment.

Without going so far as the eminent Dr. Blyden, who
asserts that 'Islam is the form that Christianity takes
in Africa,' there would certainly seem to be a greater
adaptability in the Mohammedan creed to the wants of
the African nature than exists as a rule in the dogma
of Christianity *as taught*—that is to say, European
Christianity. So strongly is this influence recognised
that a Director of Mohammedan education has been
appointed in Sierra Leone, and in the British West
African colonies state grants and official assistance
are given to the Mohammedan schools. The reason for
its popularity may be that the Mohammedan missionaries work through African teachers and ideas,
while Christian missionaries in West Africa insist on
presenting their ideas through European glasses and
generally by direct European teaching, but of the actual
fact there is little question.

For several decades now Mohammedanism has been
steadily spreading under the influence of a strong
religious revival throughout the whole of West Africa
and even down into the Congo. In another direction Mohammedanism appeals to the African native,
in that it permits polygamy, which is closely bound up
with the habits of life of the African black. In the
Lagos hinterland especially has progress been very
marked, as also in Senegal and the French Soudan
generally, while a steady campaign is also proceeding
on the Gold Coast. Mohammedanism, once listened
to by the negro, easily captures his emotional and

sentimental nature, and under the influence of his characteristics becomes a tremendous force—for good or evil. Its professors are distinguished conspicuously throughout West Africa by a dignity and self-respect differing alike from the bearing and conduct of the pagan or that of many of the professors of Christianity, though no reflection is being cast on the genuine converts to the latter.

The vast possessions of France in this part of the world are almost wholly peopled by Mohammedans, and in Senegal a vigorous propaganda is carried on down to the coast, while far away in the extreme east the Senussi missionaries are traversing Ubanghi and Baghirini and penetrating down to the Congo itself. Our neighbours have not been slow to recognise the influence for good which such a state of things may be made to exercise, and have established numerous schools at which the sons of Mohammedan chiefs receive instruction on Western lines, and special teachers appointed by the government teach Arabic together with French. By this means a set of educated Moslem chiefs are growing up, who are able to render the greatest service in the development of the country in accordance with the native sentiment but on European lines.

Turning now to paganism or fetichism, a totally different set of circumstances is of course presented to view. 'Fetish' is still the accepted religion of the greater part of the sea-coast between the Senegal and Congo, of a large part of Nigeria, and of nearly the whole of the Congo Free State, while isolated communities are found to exist throughout all the Mohammedan territories of the Western Soudan. Of the four principal schools of fetichism into which West Africa, from the Senegal to the Congo—some 3,000 miles— may be said to be divided, that existing in Southern Nigeria may be taken as a specimen, as it is the one where fetichism (or 'ju-juism') may be observed at present in its most unchanged form. As a very brief summary of this form of belief, it may be said that in the mind of the West African every animate or in-animate object has a spirit of its own; further, those who have ceased to live in the body still hover about somewhere handy to their original domicile; and, finally, that there is a large class of extra non-human spirits who have the power to interfere at will with affairs in their special departments. The universe, in fact, is composed of a multitude of spirits—some dwell in persons and things; some have done so; and some never have and never will. Man, as understood by the West African, occupies a merely incidental place among this world of spirits; the non-human spirits neither know nor care anything about the living human spirits unless the latter get in their way or inadvertently cause them offence. Notwithstanding this, however, the more powerful non-human spirits (or 'nature spirits') are always ready to render assist-ance to man for value received if he likes to propitiate them by offerings or sacrifices; hence it follows that, starting from a kind of logical pantheism, the native mind arrives at the conclusion that all spirits must be constantly propitiated to prevent them harming him, and any good service on their part must be purchased by further propitiation, which latter is always open to the objection that the spirit whose services are sought is ready to sell them to the highest bidder, so that an enemy may come along and obtain assistance against the first buyer by a superior gift. Below all this belief in different spirits with varying powers of good and evil (the native does not worry much about the good as they cannot hurt him), however, lies the original belief, forgotten now by the generality of the population, which, as Miss Kingsley very truly pointed out, is pure Brahminism, *i.e.* that all are but manifestations of the universal spirit which fills the universe.

One of the most curious features of ju-juism is the belief in trial by ordeal current throughout the length and breadth of West Africa and accepted as conclusive evidence to the guilt or innocence of the accused— death proving guilt and escape innocence. Beyond this there was formerly no appeal except to the terrible 'Long Ju-Ju.' Since the fall of the three great fetish kingdoms of Dahomey, Ashanti, and Benin, and co-existent with them, the principal seat of this dread potentate was in the Aro country in Southern Nigeria. The latter was conquered a year or so ago after a six months' arduous campaign, and the evidence found revealed that of all the pilgrims who made their way to Long Ju-Ju for a final appeal none ever returned. The Aros, with that smart commercial instinct which distinguishes West Africans, offered a few, as a kind of advertisement, to the Long Ju-Ju and kept the others as slaves. The appeal to Long Ju-Ju (and there have been, perhaps still are, several of these) was only allowed in cases of witchcraft.

The writer was once present in an official capacity at a case at Lokoja, in Northern Nigeria, arising out of one of these trials by ordeal, and some very interesting evidence was brought out. In the case in point, it appeared that the stage manager had not observed the usual traditions in such cases, and the elders of the village had therefore denounced him to the Royal Niger Company's administrator. The latter, desiring to impress on the people the illegality of these practices, had the individual in question seized and brought before him, and a whole crowd of native men and women in their long flowing Mohammedan dress crowded the court for two days, shedding in their evidence much light on trial by ordeal as carried out even in comparatively enlightened communities. The prisoner, a villager who was as old as he looked villainous and ugly, was stated to be the head slave of the late chief of the village and had occupied that position for a great number of years. The latter died suddenly, and in accordance with the general native belief, where it has not yet been completely extirpated by Mohammedanism, a search was made for the individual who had bewitched him. Hereupon the prisoner, who by local custom enjoyed absolute power until the appointment of the new chief, at once denounced the chief's sister as the guilty party. The latter appears to have been a young woman who was very popular locally and who was the inheritor of the dead man's property. Now, the universal punishment for witchcraft is death, subject only to the option of the trial by ordeal, and the latter at once claimed this privilege. A decoction of sasswood was procured, and in the presence of the village she drank it off, and a few minutes later failed to retain it, so proving her innocence and making the action harmless.[1] Here the drama

---

[1] In this connection it is interesting to note that the same ordeal is practised by the South African natives, as is shown in the section dealing with that region,

should have ended, but the head slave was for some reason or other actuated by a deadly hatred to the unfortunate girl, and, stating the draught had been tampered with by the witch-doctor, prepared another himself and insisted on a second trial. Under ordinary circumstances, as emphatically stated by the witnesses, no one, not even the chief himself, could have taken such an action, but during the interregnum the head slave's power was absolute and undefined, he being responsible to none. At any rate the accused woman, seeing no way of escape, fled into the bush and was ultimately pursued and shot by her persecutor as a witch. This, however, was not 'cricket,' and, as stated, the village elders denounced the action to the authorities. As a result it may be said the offender was found guilty and died accordingly at Lokoja during the week. One or two interesting points arose, however, during the trial. Great efforts were made to learn how it was that a deadly poison can be made into a harmless emetic, and the consensus of expert opinion seemed to be that one ' squared the witch-doctor,' but the latter, on being questioned, professed utter ignorance of any such irregular behaviour. Both the new chief of the village and the chief of the district were present at the trial in court, and were very closely cross-questioned as to their reason for not interfering at the trial by ordeal when ordered a second time. The latter cleared himself by an alibi and the former asserted that, being powerless until elected, he was prevented by the prisoner by *force majeure.* Either no men were present when the second trial was ordered or else they proved intractable, and the cross-examination had to be confined to the women. One, on being asked what took place, said

when the second draught was prepared she went outside, ' as she did not like to see people die.' There
being no evidence as to what the new chief actually
did on the occasion, the latter, a noble-looking man
having Fulah blood in his veins, was exonerated.
According to his account he was paralysed with horror ;
according to the prisoner's it was he who ordered that
the woman was to be killed at all costs.   The people
present when examined on the first day seemed to
think the latter not improbable, though this was not
said in so many words.   At the adjourned trial on
the following day their doubts had entirely disappeared,
and remarkably similar categorical statements were
made as to the heart-breaking grief of the chief at
the action.   Things being as they were then in
Northern Nigeria, the villagers were wise in their
generation ; and the one who paid the penalty, judging
from the united testimony of those who had known
him from youth, at least met his deserts justly on
general if not on specific grounds.

The Bantu fetichism, though on the same general
principles, differs in some respects very considerably
from that of the negro.   There is also a vast amount
of detail common to both relating to the different souls
a man possesses and as to the action of souls after the
death of the body, and many, if not most, of the human
sacrifices are more or less connected with this last.   However, the limits of space at the disposal of the writer
forbid further consideration of what is perhaps the most
fascinating side of native African life and character.
Those desirous of further details are referred to the
writings of Miss Kingsley, Messrs. Ellis, Dennett, and
others.

CHAPTER XV

ADMINISTRATION

BEFORE proceeding to consider the question of European administration in West Africa, a short space may be devoted to the method of self-government as existing to-day in a typical negro community, and for this purpose the Fantees of the Gold Coast may be taken as an example; though it must be borne in mind that the methods of government, even among the negro tribes, differ widely, and are multifarious in character, while among the Fulani-ruled Hausa States and similar countries the methods more resemble those obtaining in the native states of India. The following very complete description of the Fantee social organisation is taken from ' Gold Coast Native Institutions,'[1] by Caseley Hayford, a West African native barrister, well known at the Gold Coast Bar :

' Every native of the Gold Coast or Ashanti is a member of a family. He sinks or swims by the fortunes of his family. There is a community of interest amongst the members of such family, who, as a rule, trace their ancestry from a common mater-familias. The male members of such family regard the children of their sisters with peculiar feelings of kinship. The relationship existing between an uncle

Sweet & Maxwell, 3 Chancery Lane, E.C.

and a nephew or a niece is tersely expressed by the phrase, *na dzi yinaä*, meaning " he is his all in all." You have here the bed-rock basis of the native State system. Now a given community, it may be a village community or a township, consists of individual families, whose heads represent such individual families in the village or town council. So that you have here an elective system which is at once natural, and commands the confidence of the electors. In large townships you will have the different wards (being, for convenience sake, the different sections into which the community is divided) consisting of a given number of families, such wards having the right to elect their most intelligent and influential members into the town council. The heads of the families are known as *Panins* or elders, and the head of the ward is the head *Panin* or chief elder. To him all the members of the ward pay the greatest homage and respect. But how came families to be congregated together thus into wards, or into given sections, of the township? If you examine the matter carefully you will find that the original members of the ward are members of the same tribe : for it is a thing practised to this day that when a stranger enters a village or a township, and desires to become a member of the community, he finds out where the members of his tribe live, and would invariably live among them rather than dwell with a different tribe. Now since a man belongs to his father's company, and his father generally lives with the members of his family, it does indeed happen that the sons of the male members of a given ward join themselves to such ward. We have thus the beginnings of the *Arsafu* or company system, the word

Arsafu being a corruption of *Insefu*, meaning friends, and, by extension, friends in arms. A son in early life lives with his father, and, naturally, the friends of his youth would be the youth of his father's ward, and he would, therefore, as he grew to manhood, associate himself in arms with the friends of his father's ward, who together would form an *Arsafu* or company. The principal *Panins* of the ward and the principal captains of the *Arsafu* would be entitled to represent the ward at the council meetings of the township. We come next to the civil chiefs who form part of the town council. These generally represent the aristocracy of the township, in most cases their ancestors having first settled in the country with the ancestor of the king or head chief. Then comes the linguist, who is the spokesman of the king. We have thus in the council of an aboriginal township, analytically, first the king, then the *Tufuhin*, then the civil chiefs in their order of importance, then the captains according to their rank, then the linguists, then the *Panins* of the several wards. We have seen that a village council is only a miniature town council. Even so is the town council but a miniature district council, the latter being but a miniature of a provincial council, which again is a miniature of a State council, the great Parliament of the people.

' Now, to elucidate the foregoing, take for example the township of Agambra, whose stool is under that of the district of Princes, whose stool is under that of the province of Axim, whose stool is under that of the State of Ahanta. Imagine for a moment, then, that there is a big political issue affecting the whole State of Ahanta to be discussed. Notice by gong-gong would be given in every village community and township throughout the entire State. The *Panins* and captains of the wards of a township, who would be joined by the *Panins* of the village communities, would discuss the matter and arrive at a conclusion among themselves. They would next appoint the most intelligent of their number with a linguist to represent them at the council of the district, where also the matter would be discussed a second time, and a decision come to. Next, each district would send its representatives with the head linguists to the provincial council. Lastly, the several head chiefs of the provinces would attend the State council in great state, with their several principal councillors and linguists, where the king paramount would sit in solemn conclave with his vassals, and finally dispose of the matter, such *plébiscite*, of course, binding the entire State. It is a beautiful system, this wheel within wheel, which brings satisfaction to the minds of the adult members of the entire State, when any matter affecting their vital interests happens to be under discussion. When you add to this the further consideration of the almost communistic method of holding property, you have a perfect system, which, properly developed and worked, would usher in a new civilisation, the like of which the world has probably never seen.'

It will thus be seen that a complete machinery of government exists, and, owing to the powers of the council of chiefs throughout West Africa, no great abuse of the supreme power towards his own subjects can be practised by the king without their consent. As, moreover, the 'law-god' secret societies exist among all the negro and most of the Bantu tribes in West

Africa, nothing contrary to native law and custom can be carried out without raising insuperable opposition in the tribe, though where European influence has been used injudiciously to weaken native institutions this has been modified to a very large extent.

The permanent residents of West Africa being confined to the native races of the country, the methods of administration of the different colonial governments naturally affect the native alone. In the British colonies the very unsatisfactory 'Crown Colony' system obtains—a governor assisted by nominated councils, in no case in any way representative of the country at large ; or where (as in the case of Lagos) a good non-official element is present these can be—and are—outvoted, in case of opposition, by the governor and his official members. In the French colonies things are managed much better. A unified administration is in operation, as in South Africa, by the existence of a governor-general and council, with local lieutenant-governors and fairly representative local councils in each colony. In Senegal, for example, the council is elected by so much of the country as is under *direct* French (as distinct from autonomous tribal) rule—that is to say, practically speaking, by the taxpaying inhabitants and traders of the principal towns on the coast and in Lower Senegal. In the Congo Free State, in addition to the superior council to advise the king in Belgium, the governor-general has the assistance of a similar nominated body at Boma. Local conditions here do not admit at present of following the French system, but it is guided largely in its deliberations by the reports and advice of the district commissioners, who, with the co-operation of the local chiefs and their own officials, form really limited autonomous administrations.

Turning to the *local* governments in force in the various territories, we find here much variety of conditions existing, with much room for criticism in some cases and for commendation in others. The best that can be said perhaps is that every form of administration adopted by a superior to a subject race is being carried out, under (generally) expert observation and direction, and provided the vitality of the negro carries him through, we may at least begin to find out by experience the kind of government best adapted for his moral and material well-being and regeneration. Generally speaking, however, there may be said to be three main principles at work. The first is to govern the native directly by European officials on European lines; the second, to govern him on European lines indirectly by placing the carrying out of the policy in the hands of the chiefs under resident officials; and the third, which is now gradually replacing the former two, is to allow him to govern himself in his own way subject only to the general supervision of a European resident or commissioner.

In Sierra Leone and parts of the Gold Coast the former courses have been and are still too much persisted in. In the Lagos Protectorate, however, where in the past the system has been seen at its worst, Sir William MacGregor, that very able administrator, is bending all his energies to strengthen and perpetuate the native institutions and forms of government and so to make them quasi-independent autonomous provinces of the Colony. A certain amount of friction has arisen in doing so—partly with the European traders, who resent paying taxes imposed by the natives in a British territory, and partly from the fact that the governor being an exceptionally ' strong ' man has to some extent forced the second policy on the native States along with the last named, *i.e.* where to his mind the native methods are wrong, insisting on the native councils altering them in accordance with European theories. It has been, and probably always will be, a moot point whether a self-governing subject race should be allowed to develop on its own lines, under the advice of the governing power, until time educates it up to adopting the better methods of the latter, or whether it is better to force the reforms called for on it in teeth of the opposition of the moment. The writer is somewhat inclined theoretically to favour the former, but in practice it must be remembered that the latter course is often the only one possible in the interests of the development of the country and of other races.

In Southern Nigeria, the *local* administration have been also carrying out a policy of strengthening local government in every possible way. In addition to recognising the powers and courts of the chiefs, the laws of the ' house ' system have been officially sanctioned and are now even enforced by a special law. This system is rather too complicated to enter into here, but, briefly speaking, it is the association of several families, their slaves and servants, under an elected head, into a private guild, which carries on in common all trade and at the same time looks after all its members, thus doing away with pauperism and controlling the conduct of individuals.

For those interested in the government of the native Republic of Liberia, the following particulars may be given. The country, which is inhabited by some 50,000 civilised blacks and 1,500,000 or more aborigines, is governed on an American model by a president, vice-president, chairman of the senate, and cabinet of six ministers. The legislative branch comprises the senate (consisting of two representatives of each of the four counties) and a house of representatives of twenty-three members. Both houses have the right to reject each other's bills, but the senate has sole charge of foreign relations and of appointments. Liberian law extends inland from the coast settlements as far as the aborigines can be persuaded to receive it, which may be put at an average of ten to fifty miles, and in these districts commissioners represent the central authorities. Outside this area, and to a large extent within it, the tribes are under their own laws. Within the government's radius of influence the aborigines are eligible to vote on giving proof of certain civilised tendencies. A supreme court exists and bears a very fair reputation. The principle of local government has, however, received the greatest sanction in French West Africa, where it has for a number of years been given a fair trial with the best results. In their oldest colony of Senegal, that part of the country which does not elect representatives to the lieutenant-governor's council is governed locally by the tribal laws obtaining in each district, subject to French supervision, each district disposing also of its own local budget to a certain extent. A similar state of things exists in their other colonies, where circumstances permit.

Turning to the Congo Free State, the general division of the territory, from an administrative point of view, is based on the districts at the head of each of which is a district commissioner representing the State. The commissioner is assisted by sub-commissioners but is alone responsible for the good order of his district. Their principal instructions, on which the State lays great stress, are to maintain friendly relations with the natives and wherever possible to prevent or patch up intertribal disputes; they are also charged with abolishing as far as possible barbarous customs, and especially human sacrifices and cannibalism, still practised over a large extent of the territory. Among other duties may also be mentioned that of providing transport, engaging porters, and seeing that no abuses of conscripted labour are committed. Where the district is subdivided into zones these sub-commissioners are also responsible to him, as are also the commanders of the different stations in his district. In close co-operation with the district commissioner is the native chief or chiefs of the district. The institution and recognition of these are encouraged by the State in order to improve the relations between it and the natives, to consolidate authority over individuals, to ameliorate their condition, and to facilitate their regular contribution to the development of the country. The chiefs have as a rule to be first recognised as such by native custom, and are then officially recognised by the government and receive a certificate to that effect. They are allowed to exercise their usual authority according to native usage and custom, provided the same be not contrary to public order and is in accordance with the laws of the State. They are held personally responsible for their tribe's supply of public labour, as notified to them annually. The acknowledged native chiefs amount up to date to 258.

The safeguards provided by the co-operation of the chiefs and the supervision of the central authority are now on the Congo supplemented, as far as human action under such conditions can go, by a very thorough organisation of the judicial side of the government.

It has pleased many of the critical theorists who have attacked the Congo Free State to say that this latter has been established merely as a blind to the actions of the administration. It may be merely remarked that no infant struggling State is likely to go to the great expense of such an elaborate and widely organised system of justice as has now been called into existence on the Congo *pour rire*, and further-more that jurists of the character of those now serving on the Congo are not those capable of lending themselves to such practices. A certain amount of latitude must of course be made for the different conditions in individual countries, especially when in a state of savagery, but, generally speaking, the Congo tribunals do their duty as well as similar ones in British colonies.

The sovereign and government of the Congo Free State have stated over and over again that they desire justice to be rendered impartially, and that as it is necessary that offences committed by natives should not remain unpunished, so penal laws must also be applied to the whites who are guilty of illegal doings. The mere fact of having constituted a superior court of appeal with judges of different nationalities and of appointing foreign lawyers and magistrates as judges and officials of the lower courts in the interior of the country is a proof, and a more than evident guarantee, of the impartiality and seriousness of the judicial administration aimed at. The writer holds no brief for the Congo Free State, rather the contrary in fact, but, in common fairness, after a very lengthy study of its judicial machinery, laws, and decrees, and the instructions given to its officials, he finds it difficult to conceive what more King Leopold could have done to safeguard its internal affairs than has now been done—given the peculiar conditions of the country. The abuses which have from time to time arisen in the past have been due, as far as one acquainted with similar conditions in West Africa can see, to three things, viz.—to the abuse of power by agents of the concessionaire companies before the State had fully realised the necessity of keeping a sharp control over these semi-independent individuals; (2) to the want of experience of early officials; and (3) to the lack of trained colonial servants whose known antecedents and constitutions fitted them for isolated and arduous responsibility in an unhealthy tropical and savage country. It is only right to add, however, that, though isolated misdeeds may still continue to occur here as everywhere else, the measures now in force guard as far as possible against a repetition of the former regrettable occurrences, and where these occur the offenders are brought to trial without delay.

CHAPTER XVI

LAND TENURE

IT is now necessary to consider the land question, but before doing so it is worth while to consider the difference between the native and European ideas on this subject. The native idea represents that of primitive society everywhere in the world, the European that of latter-day civilisation; and, if this was only borne in mind more, less nonsense would be written by those ill-informed sentimentalists who insist on treating the former on the lines of the latter. Nothing is more astounding in regard to the present Congo campaign in this country—to take a very flagrant case in point—than the utter ignorance displayed by those who, while violently denouncing every detail of Congo administration, appear to be totally unaware either of the past history of social evolution, of modern civilisation in Europe, or of the conditions existing in other African countries at the present day.

To understand the difference referred to above, it must be borne in mind that the recognition of ' property' as such is one that has materially differed in the progress of civilisation. Briefly it may be defined, as now accepted, as a permanent right vested in a human being to absorb for his own benefit the various advantages which accrue from a physical object; and, going a step further, to use it as he pleases. The primitive idea of all races has not even admitted the first part of this definition, but has only granted a temporary communal right, and under these circumstances it may be safely asserted that property, as we know it, had no existence in the earliest primitive stage. The development of the idea of property is born of the growth of knowledge on the part of those who had the opportunity of a limited enjoyment of the benefits to be derived from it. Personal property, no doubt, was first assumed in clothes and weapons; the idea of property in land must necessarily have been of very much later growth. As a huntsman pure and simple, primitive man would have been very far from such an idea. In his next stage as a pastoral nomad, the cattle in course of time would come to be regarded as property, as well as families, and, possibly, slaves. In old times only cattle actually born to the herdsman were looked on as his actual property, and other cattle, even if obtained in war, became part of the communal property of the tribe. In the third stage, we reach that of the agricultural state of society, and, whilst property in land may here be said to arise, it will be seen to be a restricted property and very far from our modern ideas on this head. In the first stage, the tribe or nation held certain land on which they settled, or within whose bounds they definitely settled, as common property; as a more permanent state of things arose this land was divided amongst districts, and again finally amongst villages, but still held in common amongst the members of the particular community. Arrived at the 'village community' stage, two systems

were pursued ; in some countries the villagers cultivated the land utilised in common for their common
needs, in others individuals or families cultivated their
portions by themselves, but subject to the conditions
of the community as a whole. In the latter case,
though individual property would seem to be implied,
yet it was only the benefit of temporary use granted to
those who were integral parts of the community. No
power existed on the part of these individuals or
families to alienate their land to outsiders, and on
exhaustion of the land the village, in removing to
other places, took no more heed of the land abandoned.
Generally speaking, the portion so under temporary
use or cultivation bore or bears but the most insignificant proportion, in primitive society, to the uncultivated territory over which the tribe roamed or roams,
and formed temporary settlements at intervals of a
few years. Needless to say, under such conditions, if it
had been the habit of more highly cultivated races
occupying the country to consider the *whole* country
as the personal landed estate of the tribe (an idea on
the subject of property, by the by, which would be
utterly incomprehensible to a tribe in such a stage of
development), the condition of the world at large
would be at the present moment very similar to that
of savage Africa at the present day, where, it may be
remarked, all the various stages of evolution referred
to may be observed in different localities. The
absurdity and impossibility, therefore, of applying the
modern ideas of property obtaining in Europe in
exactly the same way to all these different evolutionary
states existing is at once apparent, and the mode in
which questions of land tenure should be dealt with is

far from being the simple question which our superficial would-be critics would lead us to believe.

One would naturally suppose, to listen to these gentlemen, who ' confuse counsel with a multitude of words,' that in British Possessions all native races were found in an equal state of development, and that the first act of the Imperial Government on coming into the country was to make a free gift to the individual inhabitants of every acre contained within its boundary. Is this so? Well, let us see what is the case in one particular colony. In Uganda natural conditions in many respects are very similar to those obtaining in the Congo Free State and, to a large extent, in Northern Rhodesia. On turning to the report made by Sir Harry Johnston, his Majesty's Special Commissioner, in July, 1901, we read :

' The general arrangement regarding the land settlement effected during the past eighteen months is as follows : *Where the country is inhabited by settled natives they are to retain, as individuals or tribes, in their exclusive possession the land they actually occupy or cultivate. All forests and all waste land have become the property of his Majesty's Government.* In return for the surrender of these rights to the waste and uncultivated lands, in almost all cases direct payments have been made to the chiefs or peoples. The exceptions to this rule have been few, and have been occasioned by unprovoked attacks on the part of the natives. In imposing terms of peace, these once hostile natives have been guaranteed the possession of lands they occupied, but have been told that the right to the waste and uncultivated lands has been vested in his Majesty's Government by right of conquest. In cases

where the natives surrendered their rights voluntarily
and without compensation, a promise has usually been
given that, in the event of the tribe increasing and
multiplying to a considerable extent, the local Government would endeavour to allot it further tracts from
out of the waste and uncultivated lands to meet the
increase of native population.   In the province of
Uganda and the district of Toro, where the natives had
attained a certain degree of civilisation, and where
individual ownership of land is a matter of great importance, an attempt has been made to bring about a very
elaborate allotment.   Estates have been marked off,
both large and small, by the local chiefs, in concur-
rence with the European Administration, and it is
hoped that the Uganda Survey Department may put a
seal on this settlement by a survey which would place
these boundaries beyond dispute.   I think I may say
that nothing has more tended to bring about friendlier
relations between the European Administration and
the native population than this adjustment of the land
question.   What the natives dread on the advent of
European control is that they will lose their lands
and become the tenants of European landlords.   In
the case of tribes like the Masai, who do not cultivate
the soil, or do not even settle on it very definitely,
grazing grounds to a fair extent have been allotted on
much the same lines as though the land was under
cultivation.   There are, of course, parts of the Protectorate, as I have already pointed out, absolutely without a settled population, which are only occupied
temporarily by hunters in pursuit of game or in search
of wild-bee honey.   Here the British Government has
at its disposal valuable tracts which it can open for

direct European colonisation without in any way hurting the feelings of an indigenous race. Elsewhere in the Protectorate, however, so long as the natives live loyally under our protection and pay the taxes which they have agreed to pay, great tenderness should be shown towards their feelings in regard to the land, for it is they who will, or should in the main, support the charges of the Administration. Of course there remain in these countries enormous tracts of fertile soil which the Government may deal with freely, and may hand over to European settlers and capitalists without any injury to native rights or ·aspirations at all, but we should be careful to mentally reserve at least half of this area of disposable ground for the future hoped-for increase in the native population.'

If we turn to the British possession of the Gold Coast, where the conception of landed ' property ' is in a fairly advanced state, we find that in the greater part of the colony and protectorate such a thing as individual property or private ownership is unknown. Property belongs to families, larger or smaller, as the case may be, but ever-increasing in number. Such property is managed by the head of the family for the family benefit, and as these two doctrines of succession and property must be applied together, the power will not perhaps appear so strange, for though, when a man dies, his sister's child becomes head of the family, and succeeds as such head to the property, yet the deceased's children are members of that family though occupying a very subordinate position. Throughout the greater part of the colony succession is through the female—*e.g.* when a man dies his children do not succeed, but the property is taken by the children of his sister. A native explains the

reason thus :—' My sister's children are my blood
relatives, but whether the children my wives bear are
so or not I cannot tell.' Each member of a family has
the right to select a portion of the common land for
cultivation, but cannot acquire exclusive possession
thereof, and alienation can only be effected by the
unanimous consent of the family.[1] If, however, any
member plants trees, he has an exclusive right to the
fruit thereof, but cannot transmit that right to his
descendants. The powers of the head of the family
vary with his personal influence and character, but to
him belongs the right of allowing strangers to cultivate,
receiving the fees therefor (usually consisting of a flask
of rum, a head of tobacco, and a shilling in money),
and of permitting the cutting of palm trees for wine.
When granting permission to cultivate, the privilege
of cutting oil-palms is always reserved, but the temporary tenant does not appear to be restrained from
gathering for his own use such nuts as may ripen
during his occupation. The boundaries between estates
are marked by natural objects, such as rocks, trees,
rivers, &c., but, as the memory of 'the oldest inhabitant' is the only test, boundary disputes are frequent. A man having no land of his own goes to a
neighbouring landowner, and on paying the small fee
mentioned above obtains leave to cultivate, but when
he takes off his crop he vacates the land. Estates,
however, are frequently pawned or mortgaged for

[1] In French and German West Africa absolute ownership has been
assumed over all ' vacant ' lands, but on the Gold Coast and, to a large
extent, in Lagos and its hinterland, owing to the peculiar terms on which
British paramountcy was established, this right has not been held to
exist inherently, though by special ordinances passed in each colony the
Government has not hesitated to assume such powers in particular
instances.

money lent, the pawnee or mortgagee acquiring thereby the right to use the land as his own (except that he may not cut the oil-palms) until the loan is repaid, the use of the land standing in lieu of interest. In this manner estates are frequently transferred and pass from heir to heir of the mortgagee; the mortgagor, or his representatives, retaining the right to redeem the property by repayment of the loan at any time.

The large number of leases that have lately been obtained from the native holders for purposes of gold-mining has necessarily very much deranged the system of landed property, as hitherto leases had been almost unknown and consequently special concessions ordinances have had to be passed in the colonies affected. Every such lease has to receive the sanction of the concessions court before it becomes valid, and, both in the Gold Coast and Ashanti, the concessionaires have to satisfy the government that it is for full value received and subject to the interests of the chief and tribe in general, while it must not be for a longer period than ninety-nine years. As all the land on the Gold Coast, most of it undeveloped in any way, is claimed as the property of some tribe or other, it is a moot point whether the government has done right in thus recognising these far-fetched claims. Far otherwise is done in French West Africa, on the Congo, and in most of the other British colonies.

In the Lagos hinterland an interesting period of transition has been reached, in which it is sought to adapt the changing conditions of European influence to the old native system.

The government, says a recent issue of a Lagos native paper, dealing with this subject, is evincing com-

mendable assiduity in threshing out the native land
tenure question, and steps appear to have been taken to
get the views of the native rulers of the various hinterland
districts on the subject. The result cannot be otherwise
than helpful, and it will be a gain to both the government
and the people when the usage and law governing native
land tenure are thoroughly known and understood. As
regards individual and family rights to land, these are
incontestably the basis of the system, and they found
exemplification in Lagos, under the native *régime* of
King Docemo, in the allotment of land to strangers.
When a stranger applied to the king for land the
locality in which a site was desired having been
ascertained, King Docemo would apply to the chief
who owned the locality, and request the chief to
furnish the stranger applicant with the land he
required. It was not in the power of the king to
override the rights of ownership of the chief, any more
than it is in the power of the government of a civilised
state to usurp the rights of ownership of individual
citizens. As regards the ownership rights of the chief,
these are absolute, so far as they pertain to land
belonging to himself and family, and neither the native
king nor council can deprive him of those rights or
put any limitations on them. The only difference that
exists between the ownership rights of the chiefs and
heads of families in native communities, and those
obtaining with civilised communities, is the money
value attaching to the latter, and which has led to the
introduction of a set of systems and regulations in
regard to such ownership. All the difficulty arising
in regard to native land tenure is really due to the enhanced value with which circumstances have conspired

to invest land property. It is very obvious that the circumstance of such enhanced value cannot avail to alter the rights of ownership, which are, instead, accentuated under the new order of things. This, if anything, tends to diminish rather than augment the authority of the native kings and chiefs in the premises, and the most that a native king or council can do in the way of keeping a hand on the disposal of land is by introducing a system of registration in the matter of conveyances, and requiring all such deeds to be registered. The conditions in Lagos differ materially from those of the Gold Coast, as in the former the land is more open and principally devoted to agriculture, while in the latter it is more largely covered with forests, full of valuable products, but in the interior very little worked.

In this connection reference must be made to a very important test case recently brought before the High Court of the British Central Africa Protectorate, bearing on this question of native reserves and unoccupied land. The action was brought by his Majesty's native commissioner against the Blantyre and East Africa Company, Limited, arising out of the interpretation of the clause in certificates of claim in the Protectorate which provides that natives on the land when it is bought or transferred to a European are not to be 'disturbed or removed' without the sanction in writing of his Majesty's commissioner. The Crown prosecutor held that the clause entitled the native not only to his then holding, but also to room for extension and for provision or natural increase. It was held, on the other hand, that as natives always move their gardens about, on an average once in three to five years, according to the nature of the ground, the clause provided for the safeguarding of the native so long as he occupied his original village and gardens, but did not entitle him to change his sites or take up new gardens without thereby making an agreement with the proprietor, and if the proprietor had no room for him he would then be compelled to move off on to government reserves. It will at once be seen that a most important point is raised here. The custom of European Powers taking over the administration and development of an African, and, in fact, any uncivilised, region has, as pointed out, generally been to delimit certain areas as native reserves, and so in theory to secure the native inhabitants as resident landowners and tillers of the soil for their own support. Unfortunately, experience has shown that in many cases it is only a matter of time before the majority of the native owners become a landless or, at any rate, rent-paying community. To allow the native to remain in undisturbed proprietorship, so-called, of the whole country, while only cultivating an insignificant fraction, has been found in practice since colonisation first came into existence (and as Great Britain has found in West Africa) to be utterly incompatible with any progressive development of the country, and, as his right to such is never based on anything stronger than having conquered the previous inhabitants who used to roam about its area, no valid title could in any case really be sustained for such acknowledgment of ownership over the immense stretches of territory throughout which a numerically scanty tribe is often to be found. Under these circumstances, as we have already pointed out, the sovereign power has in some form or other assumed the proprietorship or overlordship of all ' vacant ' lands, after reserving to the native inhabitants 'reserves' of greater or lesser size. In some cases, owing to the special fertility of the soil in that particular locality and the area of the reserve, no problems similar to that set forth have arisen. As a general rule, however, especially in Tropical Africa, the native's propensity for moving his village (necessitated generally by his method of husbandry, and at other times by his fondness for change) results in the original areas set aside for the wants of certain villages being in a short time abandoned, when their inhabitants, if unsuccessful in securing a fresh grant from the State, become naturally either landless nomads or rent-paying cultivators to Europeans. The question, therefore, resolves itself into what can be called 'vacant lands' and what can be considered as 'sufficient reserves;' and it is owing to the varying interpretations put upon these expressions by different powers in different colonies that their native problems may be said to arise. The judge's decision in the present case, after stating that it had already been decided *that lands not held by deed or certificate of claim are vested in the Crown since the dates of the original treaties, and that the natives are wards of the Administration and of the Courts of this country;* continues, ' We are thus brought into contact with the one great and prominent feature of the life of primitive peoples all over the world, the village community as a holder of land. It is the stage which follows the wanderings of the tribe, which generally appears first in history as a pastoral or semi-pastoral people. In theory a body of kinsmen caused by the expansion of the family, in practice containing many strangers admitted with or without ceremony of adoption, the village community is found from Russia to Fiji and from Central Africa to India and Brazil.

Here in Central Africa the village community was the political and social unit with which the Administration had to deal on the fall of the tribe, and as such it appears to be recognised in the clause in the certificate of claim. Individual ownership of land is nowhere insisted on. It is an idea which the native is only slowly beginning to appreciate. The land is not necessarily tilled in common, though this is done in many parts where all cultivate together and one large *nkokwe* or food-hut contains the whole of the village seed. It may be partitioned into lots, but the ownership or freehold and other rights or obligations are vested in the community as a whole, without right of alienation by individuals, excepting only the yearly crop. A stranger admitted into the village assumes the obligations as well as the privileges of a member of the community. The lands are not the subject of sale, barter, or mortgage to Europeans or Asiatics. They may, however, be exchanged with the Commissioner's consent. Provided that the village in question is one which, like nearly all the existing villages in this Protectorate, has been created a "native reserve," and where the land in consequence is considered to belong to the native community and cannot be alienated without the consent of the said community and of the Commissioner and Consul-General, a missionary desirous of building a church, chapel or school in any such village can do so on obtaining the village majority of the people, and on the understanding that the land on which he has built the church, chapel or school remains the property of the natives, and that the fact of his having erected a building on it gives him no claim over the site whatever.' After discussing the meaning of the word 'plantation' ('native villages and plantations,' *vide* wording of agreement), his Honour decided as follows : 'The Court therefore is of opinion that a sufficiency of land to obviate the necessity of migration, to allow of a proper rotation of gardens, and a proper fallow period for the soil according to the native system of cultivation—or absence of system—viz., at least six acres per hut, should accompany each original village. A further two acres per hut should be allowed to provide for the natural increase of the community, and no village of less than ten huts should be recognised. This calculation has been based on the evidence produced in Court, which has established the fact that the normal native garden is two acres, producing, as it were, a quantity sufficient to provide for a single family.'

We have here admitted (as in Uganda, where we have shown that it has been actually carried out) the right of the British Crown to assume ownership of 'vacant lands,' and the principle enunciated that the reserves allotted must be sufficient to allow of the lying fallow of the ground for a period of three years in addition to allowing a proportion for the natural increase of the family. Had the same principles set forth above been applied in the early days to British West Africa, that country would be far more prosperous and advanced than is the case to-day. Bearing these facts in mind it is possible to understand more fully the

situation on the Congo, where the general system has
been pursued of assuming possession of the vacant
lands and allotting to natives reserves throughout the
country, though it may be remarked that on the plea
of conquest alone the State has a valid title to a large
part of the country apart from that set forth.

So far, as stated, its action has been in accordance
with an indisputable and perfectly legal right sanctioned
by international custom and acknowledged by the
law of nations. As a general thing, the ruling power
after this contents itself with leasing out the lands to
Europeans, or where, as in many parts of West Africa,
want of labour and transport is in evidence, allowing
them temporarily to lie idle or gradually deteriorate by
native exploitation carried on irregularly. In the case
of the Congo Free State, however, the opposite course
has been taken, i.e. the State has undertaken the direct
exploitation of its private domains, the profits realised
being allotted to public works and the expenses of
administration and, without stopping to examine the
necessities of the case, its critics have eagerly seized on
this as a point of attack.

When criticisms however are raised against the very
complete system of land tenure now in existence on
the Congo as regards the State, non-natives and natives,
it is as well to remember that the *exploitation* of the
land by the State is an after and separate act quite
unconnected with the assumption of sovereign powers
over the land in the State, which latter is in accord
with general European and universal American custom,
though, after all, whether a State raises money for public
revenue by selling, leasing, or by personally exploiting

the State lands seems to be a mere matter of detail in which the principle of the action is exactly the same. *En passant* it may be remarked that the Royal Niger Company, though an administration, raised its principal revenue and paid its dividends by its trade—not by duties or taxes.

CHAPTER XVII

LABOUR

NOTWITHSTANDING the demands of the new mining industry and extension of railways, West Africa as yet cannot be said to have reached anything approaching the parlous condition of South Africa with regard to the supply of native labour, though should the first named continue to develop at its present rate another year or two may see some form of labour crisis loom on the horizon. At present, roughly speaking, the supply is equal to the demand, though the *willingness* to work of large sections of the population has yet to be demonstrated. The ordinary native, outside a few of the large coast towns, can support himself and family in affluence by an average of a day or two's work each week, at an outside estimate, and he utterly fails to see the necessity of hiring himself out for long periods to gain a superfluity of what is of no value to him. Should he wish to go in for accumulating a fortune, he can do it much more easily and profitably (in the British Colonies) by trading in the natural products of the forest than by working for Europeans. It must be borne in mind, however, that owing to centuries of internecine warfare the population of West Africa is not a large and certainly not a superfluous one, whilst the whole of the present trade of the country being in the natural products of the bush, what working energy there is is used up in this direction— very necessarily, it is true, but not leaving a large reserve to draw on for mining or public purposes. With the changed conditions of life, however, growth of European settlements and spread of education there has come into existence of late years a class of natives whose tastes require more resources and who at the same time, owing to their upbringing and residence in the coast settlements, have greater difficulty in supporting themselves. In Free Town, Sierra Leone, the result has been to turn every man into either a clerk or petty trader, eking out a scanty livelihood in a ' respectable ' but unsatisfactory manner. On the Gold Coast the same remarks apply to some extent as regards the coast towns, though this has been counter-acted to a considerable extent by the technical training provided by the missionary institutions. In Lagos town conditions are somewhat similar, only there is a considerable opening there for those described under the term ' skilled workmen.' The hinterland of the latter is a large agricultural country, but the drawing of labourers from there for railway building in other colonies has given these, on their return, a distaste for their old life, and they prefer to remain in Lagos town as ' unemployed.' The Government has now prohibited the export of any more labour from the Colony. It may be noted that a very superior professional class has been evolved all along the Coast from the better educated and cultured spirits amongst the new genera-tion under European influence. Taking the present available labour sources of West Africa as they stand,

the first place must of course be given to the ubiquitous
Kroo boy of Liberia, without whose aid the business of
the Coast could hardly be carried on. As ship and
beach boys they are unrivalled and have now become
the great stand-by of the Gold Coast mining companies.
To these natives of Liberia must also be added the
Bassa boys, who are thought very highly of for mining
purposes, as well as the Monrovia boys. In Sierra
Leone, though a certain amount of skilled labour is
available, the majority of the natives in the Free Town
district are not in love with work, except the kind
already mentioned. In the Southern (Sherboro') district, however, there are several tribes of fine physique,
such as the Gallinas, Goralis and Mendis, who not
only make excellent labourers, but are ready and willing
to go abroad annually like the Kroo and Bassa boys.
On the Gold Coast the bulk of the population—the
Fantees—not only do not 'go in' for mining, but
appear to possess a rooted aversion for every other
form of work. Southern Nigeria has sufficient labour
for local requirements, but is not likely to be in a
position to export any on account of the great natural
wealth of the country in forest products. The Hausas
in Northern Nigeria are one of the finest races in our
West African possessions, and it is hoped that their
services may be used to some extent as foremen and
superintendents by the mines. It is a pity that some
of the turbulent pagan tribes of both sections of
Nigeria cannot be shipped off for a short period to learn
habits of industry there, but public opinion in England,
which would learn unmoved of the slaughter or even
starvation of thousands, would stand aghast at using the
enforced services of intractable and rebellious idlers and

plunderers for their and our ultimate benefit. All the
same, some kind of Glen Grey Act in West Africa is
badly wanted. The French Ivory Coast is stated to
have a superabundance of labour, as also Dahomey,
but the local governments do not encourage the engagement of the natives for other colonies. Still,
should the gold industry of the Ivory Coast expand
to the dimensions prophesied it would at least have
enough for its own requirements, though the same
might be said of the Gold Coast if some system were
adopted of compelling the native to put in (for re-
muneration) a period of work each year. The result of
their present idleness, safeguarded in life and property
at our expense, is equally demoralising to the native
and unfair to his administrators, as not only is it the
duty of the citizen of each state to contribute in some
form to its development and welfare, but it is the only
way in which the moral evolution of the uncultured
savage into a civilised being is possible of attainment.

Further south, getting down to the Congo again,
we find a State which, sharing these views, has the
courage of its convictions and acts upon them, to the
great scandal of our own Exeter Hall set no doubt, but
to the very marked improvement of the native races
affected, as well as to the development and opening up
of the State. A certain proportion of the rubber (which
having been unknown to the native until the interven-
tion of the State has been reserved, as are precious
metals in other countries, as a State monopoly for
revenue purposes) is collected by the natives residing in
or adjacent to those districts, the contributions, though
paid for at the ordinary local rates, being considered
in the light of taxes paid to the State. In some

districts the natives, being alive to the benefit of trade to themselves, collect these voluntarily, but in the greater part of the area a certain amount to be brought in annually is decided upon. The price paid is fixed by the local agents at that obtaining for labour occupying a similar time, and a strict supervision is kept by higher officials over these prices, to see the full amount is paid. The efforts to introduce a currency, as all over West Africa, have not been very successful in the interior districts, and recourse has often to be had in payment either to barter or to the small brass tokens (corresponding to the brass rods of Southern Nigeria). This fact may be mentioned, as some rather ridiculous accusations against the State for not paying in coin of the realm have been recently made in the English press. Even in the more accessible Kasai district the natives will not take the latter, the writer was recently informed by a friend who had just passed through that country. It may be added that the tax is so organised that when properly imposed no native need devote more than forty hours a month to this duty. And in some districts twelve hours is found sufficient for the purpose. Of course, in its inception a certain amount of abuses have arisen in carrying this out, but since the circumscribing of the powers of local agents, the stricter supervision, the more accurate census taking, and the abolition of bonuses to the agents and commissioners, these abuses are tending to disappear. A certain amount of labour for public works is also requisitioned on the Congo, but as this cannot be considered excessive in relation to the population affected, and is, moreover, the necessity of all European powers in Africa (including

Great Britain, vide Ashanti, Transvaal, &c.), from time
to time, no special reference need be made to this
point.

With regard to present rates of labour, these vary
considerably in the different colonies, but may be said
to be steadily on the up grade.

In Sierra Leone the rate ranges from 15s. to 30s. per
month ; the rate for railway labourers is 9d. per day
and for Government carriers 1s. a day, though private
employers pay less. In Lagos the rate has been at
about 9d. per day for several years, but 1s. would be
more correct to-day ; while for the interior this rate
is always claimed as a minimum. Skilled native
labour in Lagos is paid at from 1s. 6d. to 5s. per day
and more. In the last report issued by the Southern
Nigerian Government it was stated that labour is paid
at 9d. to 1s. a day. The labour chiefly employed by
the Public Works and Marine Departments and by the
commercial firms is Kroo labour. The Kroo boy also
figures largely as a domestic servant. It is difficult to
know how we could get along without this Kroo
labour. The Kroo boy is an excellent workman and
his wage varies, except in very few exceptional cases,
from 30s. (as a headman) to 10s. per month ; he is,
of course, in addition to this, supplied with rations of
rice and beef. The Kroo boy as a rule does a honest
day's work and is always cheerful over it. The great
drawbacks to Kroo labour are, first of all, the expense
of bringing it into the Protectorate—the passage
costing 25s. each way—and secondly, the boys are very
much averse to remaining away from their country for
more than a year at a time. Cooks, washermen, &c.,
are generally procured from Lagos and the Gold Coast,

and a very much higher wage is paid to them. It is probable that the wages paid in the Protectorate are far too high as regards these people, but it must be remembered that the scale of wages was started many years ago, and it was found difficult to get good men unless the same scale was kept up, and in consequence a man who is very well paid at 30s. a month as a cook or washerman in Accra will, on coming to the Protectorate, receive wages varying from 3l. to 4l. 10s. per month. His passages to and fro have also to be met. Other wages: Native clerks, 24l. to 250l. per annum; engineers, 36l. to 96l. per annum; artificers, 36l. to 150l. per annum; tailors, 30l. to 70l. per annum; carpenters, 30l. to 50l. per annum, &c., &c.

At the Gold Coast mines rates range from 1s. 3d. to 2s. per day, and in case of skilled men go much higher, as there is considerable competition.

CHAPTER XVIII

MISSIONS AND EDUCATION

THE subject of Christian missions in West Africa is very similar to that in South Africa. In both countries it is on more or less savage and uncultured pagan communities that missionary effort has to be brought to bear. The superior races of the West African *hinterland* mostly profess Mohammedanism, and have not so far, except for a certain amount of experimental propaganda among the Hausas and Nupés, been the subject of attack by Christian missionary effort. The *raison d'être* of their propaganda it is not necessary to discuss here, but some statistics of their progress and educative work may be of interest.

The Church Missionary Society first entered the field, in Sierra Leone, in 1804, and very good work was done during the first half of the century amongst the freed slaves. In 1852 the bishopric of Sierra Leone was founded, and in 1862 the Sierra Leone church was organised on an independent basis and has since undertaken the charge of its own pastors, churches and schools. The Society, however, still retains charge of the Fourah Bay training college, the grammar school, and the Annie Walsh school for girls. One hundred and ten clergymen have been ordained by the Society on the Coast. The Society's efforts were extended to

Lagos in 1845, and a native church is also now organised at that town, with a training institution at Oyo. The Lagos *hinterland* (Yoruba country) forms part of the diocese of ' Western Equatorial Africa ' ; three native assistant-bishops assist the English bishop of this diocese, which embraces both Northern and Southern Nigeria. The stations on the Niger Delta have formed themselves into a separate partially independent body, called the Delta Pastorate, but are under the episcopal supervision of the native bishop on the Niger. In 1901 the Society's missions in West Africa comprised 60 native clergy, 308 native lay agents, 29,000 adherents, 12,000 communicants, and included 137 schools with 9,000 scholars. The Anglican Church had in that year no schools on the Gold Coast and only two places of worship, the Wesleyan and Basle missions being the strongest here.

The Wesleyan Missionary Society has four mission districts in West Africa—viz., on the Gambia, in the Colony and hinterland of Sierra Leone, in the Gold Coast and Ashanti, and in Lagos, Dahomey and Togoland. In 1901 it possessed 199 churches, 61 missionaries and native pastors, 17,500 fully accredited church members, 22,000 scholars, and a Christian community estimated at 62,000. Of the churches no fewer than 112 are situated on the Gold Coast, where the Society had in the same year 42 schools in receipt of the Government grant. Considerable attention is given to technical training, and missions have also been established in the mining centres.

The Roman Catholic missions are doing some of the most useful work at the present day throughout West Africa. On the Gold Coast their headquarters are at Cape Coast Castle, where they have 1,100 members and 486 scholars; Elmina, 2,550 members and 450 scholars; Saltpond, 460 members, 285 scholars; and also stations with schools at Adjuah, Anamaboe, and Kwitta. Twelve schools are in receipt of the Government grant on the Gold Coast; three in Sierra Leone (including a high school for secondary education); and several in Lagos. The Roman Catholic missionary work in Nigeria deserves special mention.

The well-known Basle (German Lutheran) Mission on the Gold Coast is famous for the technical training its pupils receive. The headquarters are at Akrapong with a number of well-equipped sub-stations, including one at Kumasi. The Mission also possesses three well-organised girls' institutions, four grammar schools and two training-schools. The latest statistics in the writer's possession give 11 head stations; 163 out-stations; 29 ordained European missionaries; 25 ordained natives; 120 catechists; 110 teachers; 17,000 members of congregation; 7,250 communicants; 375 students in training and grammar schools, and 4,610 in elementary schools. Some 61 of their schools earned the Government grant in 1901.

The Baptists are not very prominent in West Africa, except in Liberia, where an African Baptist church of American origin is in existence. They also have stations on the Congo.

The North German (Bremen) Mission also may be mentioned as operating on the Gold Coast—a relic of the days when the Brandenburgers had forts on the coast. Statistics give 4 head stations, 30 out-stations, 66 teachers, 2,257 scholars, and 11 missionaries. Three schools earned the Government grant in 1901.

Turning to education as a whole, the system as recognised by the Government varies in each colony. On the Gold Coast there are two classes of schools, Government and assisted, numbering in 1901, 7 and 128 respectively, the latter being schools supported by the missionaries earning the Government grant. In Southern Nigeria only missionary primary schools exist, and with the exception of a Government institution started a year or two since at Bonny for combining primary and industrial education. In Lagos there were in 1901 33 schools of which 5 were secondary and, in addition, two night schools, one of which is for technical training. There is also a special Government technical school. In Sierra Leone there are no Government schools, the system of education being entirely denominational, some 77 receiving grants in aid. In 1901 there were 8,060 children on the rolls. In addition to these, six denominational schools for secondary education are in existence, totalling 807 pupils. Besides the above, Fourah Bay College (already referred to), which is affiliated to Dublin University, offers facilities to young men desirous of obtaining the B.A. degree and the licence in theology. The number of students is between 40 and 50.

Provision was made in the ' Education Rules, 1899,' by which any of the religious denominations possessing facilities for doing so, might, subject to the approval of the Government, undertake the theoretical and practical training of teachers of elementary schools. Fourah Bay College, established by the Church Missionary Society, is the institution that has, at present, been approved. A capitation grant, depending to a small extent on the result of examination, is given for each student in training, a minimum sum being guaranteed for the up-keep of the department. Candidates for admission are pupil teachers of three years' standing, or other persons approved by the Board of Education. There is also a Diocesan Technical School, open to pupils of all denominations, receiving an annual grant-in-aid from the Government. It is not largely patronised as yet, though it has been established for nearly eight years, and, in a limited way, has done good work. This is being reorganised with a view to broadening the management and widening the scope of its work.

In the small colony of the Gambia there are six mission schools receiving grants-in-aid from the Government, and the total of scholars is 1,000.

Liberia has an important college conducted under American influence and on American lines, and a number of denominational schools under American missionaries and native pastors. In the Congo Free State statistics with regard to the missions are as follows :—*Catholics* : churches, 13 ; missionaries, 160 men and 84 women ; stations, 44 ; schools, 25 ; members, 18,973 ; scholars, 5,515. *Protestants* : churches, 8 ; missionaries, 221 ; stations, 40 ; communicants, 6,521 ; scholars (week-day), 10,162 ; scholars (Sunday-school), 5,641. The principal subdivisions of the latter section are : the Baptist Missionary Society, American Baptists Union, the Wesleyan Missions and a number of American missions. All these missions possess considerable resources and their members are numerous. The British Baptist Mission, which is the oldest, has remained the strongest, with those of the American Baptists, of the Balolo and of the International Mission Alliance. Assistance is rendered to the missions by the

State Government by giving them the enjoyment of the land necessary for cultivation and by granting subsidies or reduced taxes, and considerable help is afforded by local officials where the opportunity arises.

Reverting in conclusion to the question of Christianity's influence in West Africa, it certainly seems disheartening at first sight to reflect that the total number of converts to Christianity between the Senegal and Congo is less than 250,000. Still, and notwithstanding a certain negligible proportion among these, there remains included in this body what, to use the scriptural expression, may be described as the salt of the community leavening and uplifting the great mass of the population at large, almost invisibly perhaps and certainly slowly, but none the less surely and permanently. To sum up the position in a word, the white man, whilst imposing on the native his advanced and superior civilisation, is at the same time destroying the old restraining beliefs of native morality and character. It is for the missionary to replace these by a higher teaching and rule of life reconstructing the spiritual ideals of the native and helping to lift him upward and onward to that higher stage in human development which, alike with the rest of the world, one day he is, we cannot doubt, destined by Providence to tread.